Songs of the Broken Bone

DIANE HELMAN

Songs of the Broken Bone

by Diane Helman

Copyright © 2018 by Diane Helman

ISBN: 9781730917592

Published by

Spring Mill Publishing

Sharpsburg, Maryland 21782 USA

Editing by James Bryson / jameslbryson@gmail.com

Graphics & Layout by Diane Helman / songsofthebrokenbone@gmail.com

Behold, You desire truth in the innermost being,
And in the hidden part You will make me know wisdom.
Purify me with hyssop, and I shall be clean;
Wash me, and I shall be whiter than snow.
Make me to hear joy and gladness,
Let the bones which You have broken rejoice.

Psalm 51:6-8 NASB

DEDICATION

To Nick, who will always have my yes,

To my children, who have taught me more about the Father
than I could ever have imagined,

and to the koinonia of His church, forever.

CONTENTS

ACKNOWLEDGEMENTS

Nick, you have always made me free. Loving you and building our life together is my deepest joy. You are my strong side. I am proud to be your wife.

Aly, Dax and Thijs: You are incredible creations with strong, powerful hearts. May you always choose to love all well and to be yourselves. Daddy and I love you so big!

Dad and Mom Eberly: From my youngest moment, you believed me capable and smart. You trusted me young and loved me in all the hardest ways. And to this day, you are still my greatest heroes. You always will be.

Dad and Mom Helman: Your love is never just words—it comes with everything you are and have. I am so grateful to have been added to your family.

Mark and Dawn Durniak, Randy and Corey Strombeck, Steve and Gina Burris—thank you for hanging in, always, for as long as it takes. Much of what is written here was pioneered in your hearts and on your shoulders. Thank you. Nick and I love you deeply.

Jim Bryson for your valuable expertise, and for being unveiled in your conviction that this book should exist. You helped me believe. Jacqueline, thank you for being the soft and strong backbone to this and so many projects.

Niki Wright with Just Wright Photography for the back cover photo. Your lens captures what your heart sees.

FOREWORDS

By Mark Durniak:

There are voices that bring attention to themselves. What they say and how they say it give us the ability to acknowledge and identify with their greatness, passion and purpose.

There are voices that bring attention to causes. Their echoing cry within us rallies us to battle lines on which we would lay our lives down.

And then there are voices that awaken us to ourselves. Their resonating sound, like the final tumbler in a lock, reveal depths within us we didn't know were there.

It is the voice of Father God harmonizing with His spirit DNA spoken into us at the moment of our creation.

This voice is in the writing of Diane Helman.

Though there be no direct scriptural proof, it has been an assertion of mine that every thought God has becomes a person. When we realize this, the goal is to spend the rest of our lives convincing the world of the thought He had.

Diane's writing brings glaring clarity to this original thought deep within each of us. It calls us to attention. To a lens-clearing awareness of our "Why?" and the Father who put such a holy thought there.

That thought inspires the focused and irritates the prodigal. We need voices that shake us awake and remind us of our origin. We need voices whose sounds are markers along the highway of holiness.

For many years I had encouraged Diane to write and keep writing because I saw the burrowing and incendiary potential therein. Often she eschewed such prodding thinking there were other ways to effectively impact her generation. This happens to many of us - our powerful gifts shrouded in the darkness of familiarity.

So she continued to write, grumbling at times at the lack of attention to her heart's work. But write she did. And what has come forth is a love child born of one's spirit intentionally connecting with God's Spirit. When this connection takes place, fruit comes forth. Every one of us has this same potential to bring forth "children" as the result of our union with Him. Diane's writing is the product of deep intimacy with her Jesus. And we all get to benefit from their offspring.

My encouragement to you, the reader: take your time with this book. It is broken up differently than most you have read before. Diane and the Lord together have already "cut up" your food so you can chew it without choking. Meat requires it. Chew slowly with your spirit, savoring the flavor of who He is. If you do, you will undoubtedly feel the rumbling within - the churning of your sonship, longing for manifestation.

Thank you for writing Diane. Don't stop. May this book only be the shallows of the vast depths of living water within you. I love you and I will never stop believing in you.

Mark Durniak
Senior Pastor
World Harvest Outreach

By Jim Bryson:

Diane Helman is amazing. There is no other word for the passion that lurks just beneath the surface of eyes crackling with intelligence. She takes life as it comes, yet refuses to back down when challenged, accepting nothing less than excellence. She'll take the lumps, the cuts, the bruises, the broken bones if necessary, all to come out on top, having first triumphed over her own iniquities and only afterward considering the shortfalls of others, viewing all things through the love of the Father.

These stories chronicle her journey into the known and unknown, the expected and unexpected, the blessings and the smackdowns. They are the tears of a mother; the dreams of a daughter; the heart of a wife; the laughter of a friend, and above all, the heart of a child of God content to rest at his feet, race at his side, and lead at his command. Diane writes bravely. They are stories of fear discovered and vanquished, failure met and dispatched, bloody steps to redemption, and a heart broken for love's resurgence.

Diane pulls no punches, not in life nor in print. Her stories are just as raw as she lives. This is not a theological discourse. Those looking for fluffy devotionals need look elsewhere. This is a blood-bought testament of a woman who finds herself again and again flung to the feet of God, crying for redemption, only to be lifted higher than she ever imagined.

For every person who has plunged weathered hands into a soul; who has lifted a heavy burden; who has carried a broken man; who has run the race and come up short, vowing to run another day and lead others: These stories are for you. They will carry you across the finish line.

There is nothing hidden that shall not be revealed. There is nothing in these writings that denies entrance to the human condition. Get ready for the real—the visible and invisible, shadowlands and Spirit. Take the plunge. You have nothing to lose but that which needs to be shed.

Life starts here. Jesus bought it. We live it. Diane writes it.

Jim Bryson
Spring Mill Publishing
Sharpsburg, MD

INTRODUCTION

For me, writing comes in spontaneous bursts, compelled by the seed of a thought that tumbles over into paragraphs before my mind can catch up with my heart. Thank goodness my fingers can keep up. Writing allows me to sort out my insides.

This book is a collection of the things I wrote over the course of the last few years, as I laid my heart and trophies down in the deep hunger to be my Father's daughter—not just in theory, but to live a life of His real life. Had I known the turmoil and emotional cliffs I would fall from, I may never have begun. When I found David's thoughts in Psalm 51 that read, *may the broken bones rejoice,* I instantly recognized that cry.

I know the tender, painful love song that a broken bone sings.

It's this song of love in the middle of the breaking that has taught me to trust and to rise again. We are recognized in the heavens as His own when the deaths of the old things inside cannot hold us down. And all our lives, this rebirth from death to life in every fiber of us will continue. His love will never fail to be enough to resurrect us.

The Father is willing to break, reshape, remove, heal, or even flat destroy anything that is hindering us from the life He promised us. Other than our free will to say no, He is unstoppable from complete restoration. It's His joy and our greatest thrill.

It's a road we can entirely trust Him to guide us on. Some of the things here are ideas He could only show me when the soil was wide open and ready to listen.

So yes, He scrubs me and breaks me—and continues, to this day, to refine every thing within me. I'm learning not to resist; love is a precious way to breathe. It is a starkly naked yet entirely secure, powerful existence.

And yes, without question, it is entirely worth it.

I-XXV

I

I sat down to think about something that was on my heart.
I furrowed my brow.

"Ah," He said.
"I see that you are serious.
But do you seek knowledge,
or are you looking for Me?"

I made lists, became purposeful, and worked hard.
I rejoiced to be so productive.
"Ah," He said.
"I see that you are busy.
But are you merely useful,
or are you overflowing with Me?"

I sat back and enjoyed some down time.
I ignored my phone and my responsibilities.
"Ah," He said.
"I see that you are still.
Is this laziness?
If it's rest you're looking for, it's Me."

I played, and He asked if it was pure.
I mourned, and He asked if I trusted.
I gave, and He asked if it reflected my faith.
I saw He asked not from demand, but because He loves.

He was relentless.
In every place, He examined me.
He saw me fully, refusing to celebrate the incomplete or
artificial.

I wanted to whine that His standard was too high,
that I was entitled to His affection,
but not His correction.

But I found His wisdom came with freedom.

I have seen and tasted that those He loves, He disciplines.
I have seen and tasted how His discipline expands my
freedom.

II

Jesus is willing to tear down perfectly good things inside of
us if they weren't built on Him.

Lots of us have beliefs inside we built of bible but not of
Jesus. Those things are ghosts and shells of what they were
intended, strapped together by behaviors and pretending and
rules. They aren't the powerful, inevitable fruit of having
been with Him.

They need to come down. Don't let that make you afraid.
Just let Him do what He wants to do. He's a genius and He
loves us so perfectly. His grace will get the job done; His
loving-kindness is faithful.

It's Love that wants to destroy what needs rebuilt, this time
by His reality at work—stronger, lovelier and full of
powerful love and freedom. Custom built to suit you, not
cheap or crooked. It's a house of Jesus alive in your bones,
anointing seeping from its joints, held together by Spirit.

And it's absolutely
Entirely
Completely worth
The rebuild.

III

Father
If anything in me is frail and powerless,
hungry for validation
constructed from lies and held together by fear,

by Your Spirit, burn it down.

I mean it.
Strike up Your Spirit as a match and
burn it to the ground.

I choose You over anything in me that obstructs the view
from My seat in Jesus at Your right hand.

Nothing You build in me is ever hungry for man's
validation.

A queen does not live in a shack.

Starve anything in me that is too weak to stand under the
weight of who You say we are together.

Give me discernment
to humbly submit and powerfully stand

simultaneously.

IV

There can be a cathartic effect in being raw and honest, especially if it took us a while to muster our courage. But if we want to know peace and healing in these places, let's persistently pursue truth in all our honesty.

We can't stop at being honest.

We have to push through until Truth resets our honesty.

We push through until we know Him in that place.

When we hungrily look for Jesus, rawness and honesty can prime the ground for new seed, like a hoe in a garden. He can change us and lift us up from the mud. Power and life can spring up within, germinated by the light.

Otherwise, the rush of honesty is a purely emotional release that can be easily overcome by an empty sadness that lays heavy on us. In this place, our turmoil and confusion can be worse than ever.

Rawness isn't truth. Jesus is.

Rawness isn't our healing. Jesus is.

V

There is no detail of what is going on within me
that Jesus did not encounter,
does not understand,
or did not overcome.

VI

Though many options were before me,
I gave myself only one.
And I took my heart there,
emptying it like a purse before Him.

All the anger, confusion, impatience, and pain spilled out,
the currency of flesh exchanged for His Spirit
and I gazed at Him, waiting.

Waiting for what he always did—
helping me to see differently.
Showing me what I was overlooking.
Transforming my thoughts and heart
to see all instead of part.

But this time was different.

He held my gaze and His words were simple:
"I agree. I'm working on it."

I always thought it would feel better
for Him to just agree with me for once,
instead of the hard lessons,
instead of learning to see and walk as a daughter.

But to actually come to Him
aligned in right perspective
was harder and heavier.

There was no leaving "my stuff" at His feet this time.

No lighthearted end
no healed resolutions

no feeling better
no change.

There was only Him and His perfect patience,
His desire for a friend in that place.

To be with Him there,
I had to give up the outcome I so wanted to hurry along
and trust His love to be enough.

He was going to stay, faithful and invested

until the thing was truly and perfectly completed by love,
not flesh.

It is who He is
and He will not deny Himself.

Unwilling that He should build a church
I was too impatient to surrender myself for,
I took the seat beside Him,
took His hand,
and prized His heart over my own.

It was then that my burden lifted.

His burden is light.
His love is enough.

My heart is forever nestled in His.

VII

I once read an article about a woman who changed entirely the way she lived after she was featured for six weeks on a prominent national TV series.

She changed everything. Her hair, her clothes, her mannerisms, the way she expressed herself. She became more outspoken and overcame several severe social anxieties.

When asked by a journalist what had brought on the drastic changes, she remarked that in watching herself on TV, she didn't like what she saw. She was nauseated by the timid, insecure, mouse-like creature she appeared to be, always complaining, pessimistic and small. What's more: The camera was right, and for the first time, she saw the life she had accepted.

So, she said, I decided to become who I wanted to be.

I wonder what we might finally find the will to overcome if a camera followed us around for a while.

What might the heart within us finally demand to release?

VIII

I don't think we will get very far with the big things we hope for if we are double-minded about our heart.

Many of us see big things, feel deep pulls, and we know we are being invited into Him,

away from the noise,

To be set apart.
To be consecrated and rooted entirely in His sufficiency.
To starve all things except that for which He is perfect bread.
To overcome every lie that warps His perfect Truth.
To be ignited.

Yet to pay the price seems negotiable, or at least, something we could procrastinate a little longer. Surely we can stay in the matrix another day or two.

And we can. We can opt to procrastinate our entire life. We can lay down at the end of our days, dead many years before, having ignored it entirely. Having enjoyed every detour.

But I think of how Jesus must have felt as he walked out of the wilderness. His heart entirely free, His spirit clear and burning, His mind focused, His authority pulsing under His feet and in His fingertips.

His Father's ready Son.

What would it be like to shake the mess of the world's system off our shoulders entirely...and begin?

What would it be like to walk back into a system that once distracted us, and to rip it from top to bottom in a burst of His light?

What would it be like to see the glassy stare melt from eyes and faces? What would it be like to wash them, heal them, feed them, free them? To partner with the crystal voice of Spirit in our hearts and in our community?

I bet it'd be worth anything it cost. I bet the cost would quickly evaporate at the sound of His mighty wind.

He is eager. He is calling.

IX

Sometimes, keeping myself knit with Jesus is like holding antiseptic flat to my heart.

X

It was in my heart to say,
it was on my tongue to say,
but I didn't say it.

Because I didn't know how you would hear it.
Because I feared what you would think.
Because I wasn't in the mood to be misunderstood.

So here I am,
hiding who I am,
self-assigned to loneliness,
imprisoned by mistrust.

And there you are,
forced to live without me,
wondering where I've been,
while I convince myself it's your fault.

XI

To give to someone the unadulterated truth of your heart is
an act of courage. For a son, the consequences of such
nakedness are not a matter of fear but opportunity.

XII

I disagreed.
So violently that my face burned hot.
The issue sat between us, fat and stubborn.

But you were too far away.
You and your stupid opinion were too far away.
You and your stupid side and your wrongness.

You were too far away.
You and that piece of Him you carry.

Was there any hill worthy enough to divide you from me?
Did I even have the right to tear apart the body of Jesus?

He broke Himself to save it, and here I was, too right to
care.

I wonder if the Bible writers ever intended their writings to
divide people instead of compelling the maturity that unites
them?

The flesh divides.
The Spirit contends.

He in you, and He in me,
two non-negotiable portions of His realness.
Non-negotiable.

I don't get to believe things that allow me to discard people.
Contend for them? Yes.

Discard them?

Never.

XIII
REST STUBBORNLY

Heavy heart
I am out of energy to coax you upward
I have wrestled you
all day long
and you fight back
as though you know something I do not

Help me
I hear myself crying out
but will not allow my lips to say the words
There is no one to say them to but One

All of men sit in one of two places
Flesh, they who would stroke my ego

Or Spirit, they who would say what I already know
and cannot bear to rehear

Heart, hearken to me
There is steel in this
I will not negotiate with you
You will not betray yourself

The strong blood of this Daughter runs pure

I will not short-circuit my trust of my Father
in my haste to feel better
Even now his chesed reaches out to me in thick layers
wafting with warm aromas over my hungry lonely heart

I will not give voice to fear and heaviness
and permit it to live

I will not lend power to lies
Even they know who I am

They stick and poke me that I might complain
and yield them life with my breath

But I am no fool

Voice, I will limit you to the sounds a daughter makes

I will call the Name I know
I will whisper through the heaviness
and turn my heart and remind it to trust
Implicitly trust
Without reserve, trust
So fully
that fear becomes annoyed by invincible identity
and slides away, embarrassed in its impotence

I will not betray my Father in my weak moment
This heart, though heavy, is His and always is
It is pure and true and steady
And heavy
He will find in me a true love
He will glow to find fidelity in me

I am one of His favorites
Today it is costly to keep my place

Heart, stay your rest

Heart, you will heed the word of the daughter
Rest is learned here
Rest is for this moment
Heavy heart, lay yourself down upon Rest
and be still

Hearken to the breath of this daughter
her Father's breath as she speaks now
The true sound
Therein lies your direction

Be made upon the Center of Him
and lie still
Rest stubbornly

XIV

I knew I should but I didn't want to.
I knew it was important but *'eh.*

So I turned to Jesus, gave Him my "not-want-to"
and asked Him to change my heart.

Then I started anyway,
with an empty tank of "want-to,"
with the faith that I could tap into His "want-to."

Now I want to. I don't know when it changed.

Except that at some moment, it became less about my
"want-to" and more about His.

XV

Recently, I was in the car heading to a lunch date and I felt abnormally awkward. I came to a red light and started to pray out loud, asking the Father what was going on in my heart.

Instantly, I heard: "You don't trust her."

Unfiltered, I shot back: "Should I?", thinking of all the reasons I could count as proof that my feelings were warranted.

But before I could even start listing my evidence, the Father answered with tremendous authority, a heavy sound of justice: "I do."

And He flooded my mind with the things I knew this person was entrusted with. Deep, heavy, priceless things. I was instantly aware that I had taken a foolish, arrogant stand against the heart of my Father.

The light turned green and I drove through the intersection, instantly repentant and disciplined by the Lord. I realized again how just He is. He acted as a good defender for the one I had wrongly accused, contending in love to bring me into right thinking.

This is what the Father's justice does. It burns down fleshly judgments and comes to the defense of our heavenly identity. I love seeing how He rushed to their defense--and my reconciliation to His heart--in one private moment at a red light. He's so good.

And so was that lunch date.

XVI

Son, don't for one minute fool yourself into thinking I have made peace with your decision to choose the broken way. I could never compromise My heart for your life.

I will always contend for your holiness. I am resolutely set in My love covenant with you.

If you do not hear My voice in your spirit, faithfully calling you out of your sin, it says more about your position than Mine.

I long for your contrite, clean heart.

XVII

If you're stuck in old behaviors of expressing yourself just because you think it's what everyone expects, it's time to shed your assumptions. Go ahead and change. Give others time to recover from whiplash. Embrace the awkward middle.

At some point you just have to be you and let everyone catch up.

XVIII

This morning, as we were walking out the door, Dax gently pulled Thijs aside. Thijs fussed, trying to free himself with a loud wail.

Dax held him firmly, saying to him: "Ladies first, Thijs. Ladies first," and made way for Aly and me to leave the house first.

Thijs kept wailing, insulted to be restrained by his brother. More offended than submitted. More stubborn than teachable.

I looked at Thijs and smiled: "Dax is right, buddy. He's teaching you. He's being a good brother. You are strong gentlemen! Listen to him."

With my words, Thijs immediately stopped wailing and stood quietly for his turn.

As I buckled Thijs into the van, I wondered how often my heart is closed to the voice of my Father simply because I don't want to submit to His voice in others.

How often do I foolishly stand against His heart, revealed in His sons, too arrogant to hear or too offended to see?

XIX

It's amazing how much you can learn when you lay down the urge to prove how much you already know.

XX

Live in Me.
Draw everything of life from Me.

The counsel of evil will detour you.
The way of evil will cripple you.
Any other source will oppress you.
Any other source is death for you.

But *My* law is love.
Let Me fascinate and renovate you.
The more time you spend in Me,
The more I feed your soul.

You will be fully persuaded
that you are fully alive.

What I know about you will finally become real to you.

You will be like a tree, tall and strong.
You will drink of My presence.
The things that come from you will carry My DNA.
You will endure and overcome.

Everything you do will bear fruit and prosper.

This is how you know you're sourced by Me.
This is how you know.

XXI

The most heartbreaking part about being trapped
in broken beliefs about our identity
is that it forces us to be lonely.

Because of what we see
and how we see,
we resist what is real
and cope with masks,

every inward need unmet
every inward strength wasted

and in our deepest, most precious
places of value and purpose,
we feel alone and unclaimed.

Yearning and aching,
sometimes relieved for seasons,
but always, the cycle.

Loved and then left.
No one with us who hasn't
or won't eventually
leave

or if they don't,
we do the fading.

Some reason, some cause, some excuse
some offense, some other door
championed over relationship.

It's criminal to watch
free will at its worst,

such precious divine humanity
locked in perpetual isolation by pride or fear,

blind to the ones who
really do
see and love it all with bleeding hearts,

who see the divine in the disorder,
loving the ugly with the beautiful

loving into life and staying
with fire and water and forever.

XXII

When I fixate on the pain of maturing, I am focused on the
flesh, and maturity will not result. I will just take another lap,
repeating the same struggles and conflicts over and over.

When I set my eyes on my Father and view everything
through Him, I fixate on the Spirit and maturity results,
because He puts my experiences into context.

Pain is inevitable as He matures me. But when He is my
entire context, pain cannot propel me out of rest. When pain
meets me, it will see me lean further into Him as the root of
my soul.

Maturity is being produced in me when my Father, not my
pain, is obvious to all who encounter me; when He is so
alive in me that, like Stephen, not even the pain of death can
make my eyes leave His.

XXIII

Love that begins
and then pauses for reciprocation
is veiled trade.

"I have extended myself far enough," we say,
believing ourselves hemmed by wise boundary.

"Until you give back enough
to make my expressions feel valued,
until you relieve the costs of my risk,
until you validate my heart,
until you return some treasure,

then I will love you more."

And yet, our Father's perfect love
is on full stream all the time.
His grace is best shown when love is generous
beyond all apparent merit or ability.

We are alive and at home,
the body of our Father's house.
A healed home established by love's gift.
A holy temple by heart in truth and spirit.

Is this now a place of business?
Must you give me five coins for this lamb?

Love is not for reciprocation.
Love is for response.
It invites.

Braid a whip and drive out the moneychangers.
They only restrain love's most potent expressions.

Don't focus on if they texted back;
If they understood your smile, your hug, your word;
If they seem to value your foolish, affectionate attentions;
If they misunderstand your strength;
If you sense awkwardness, restraint or even judgment.

Just do what Jesus does.

Love anyway.
Give yourself.
Give the love He gave you.

Let it invite them into the places of Jesus
for which you exist to show them.

XXIV

If, in my alone time with my Father,
I truly want to connect with Him,
I have to come as myself.

I can't come as anyone else.
I'm not Eve in the garden, camouflaged.

No, it's me He loves like crazy.
The me He made from His imagination.
The me He's jealous for.
The me that has no concept of shame.

So I walk in boldly,
pausing at the door of Jesus
to once again be washed of any ideas
of who I think I should be,
or who I might wish I was.

I come as me.

When I come as me,
I set the stage for Him
to be Himself.

Turns out the leaves that hide my vulnerability
also frustrate our intimacy.

If I want to really see Him,
I have to let Him see me.

It's me that He gave eyes to.
Any other mask blinds me.

XXV

It is unfortunately common for me to have disgruntled arguments with people when they are not in the room. I have made my case with more people in the shower, at the steering wheel, and in my kitchen than I care to admit.

Conversations I did not feel I could have with people, I would have with myself, defending against charges not made and expressing frustrations I did not have the courage to expose.

But instead of bringing freedom and relief, I found myself believing my perceptions, and they grew harder and larger, like tumors choking my relationships.

Recently, I repented of this to the Lord and promised that every time I began one of those conversations with an invisible defendant, I would have that talk with Him. He would open for me a new way. In this, He has brought me wide new avenues of maturity.

Coming to the Lord for these arguments is a habit that has taken a while to shift, and still requires a conscious decision.

I was midstream in a private rant this morning before I caught my thoughts and stopped mid-stride. I turned my heart to the Lord, instantly repentant, and laid down the arrest warrant I had written.

After I dropped off the kids, I thought again of this moment and asked Him what was happening in my heart. Instead of answering, He laid before me that which had triggered my tirade, and He made one adjustment.

He shifted how I saw myself in the situation. The moment I saw myself rightly, everything else was placed in right context. Not only was there healing but also tremendous opportunity.

All this to say: Spend time with the Father. He is the only one who can show you all things as they truly are.

XXVI-L

XXVI
IMAGINARY CONVERSATIONS

Have you ever had a conversation with someone who isn't
in the room?

Like, you're engaging them in your head,
sparing and defending
projecting their responses
through your own judgments,
entertaining the fantasy that they are entirely wrong
and you are entirely right.

I do that a lot.
Not on purpose.
It just happens when I let my mind drift.

I can always tell what's really going on inside of me
if I'm arguing with someone in my head.

I hear their imagined words in my head
arguments spawned out of my heartache
and I answer them audibly
over my steering wheel
over my dishes.

Often my kids say,
"Mama, who are you talking to?"

I lie and I tell the truth
"Myself," I say.

In that moment,
I am full of confusion and heartache.

Paul calls these moments *logismos*:
Vain imaginations
Speculations
Bitter bricks that inner fortresses are made of.

Speculations are castles of strongholds we build with lies.

I have built cities in my heart before I realized I had cast the
first stone.

They are contrary to the Spirit,
stealing and scheming and dividing
Piling layers of fat and sluggishness
on my precious and perfect spirit.

Paul is unflinchingly strong
these illusions be destroyed.

All my suspicious speculations merely reflect
where I do not yet know His realness,
or I do not yet trust others
or myself.

Healthy daughters do not prefer imagined conversations to
real ones.

XXVII

Lack of capacity = lack of intimacy

XXVIII

And there, the paths converged, coming together at a huge stone wall with many doors.

Travelers on their respective paths paused here at the doors. Some were puzzled, others confident, still others crestfallen. Which one should they choose?

There was a grand wide door... a sleek modern door... a dramatic red door with a gleaming handle...a dull grey door with cheap fixtures...

And so, travelers would pause and choose their way in a gambled decision.

Apart from all these was a door that looked like an afterthought, as though a caretaker might use it. It was smaller and heavy, as old as the wall itself, with a solid handle but no lock. It was unimpressive and few noticed it, much less considered it.

I watched the travelers come, choose, and go. They seemed to be going in circles. The lady with the candy-colored coat chose the red door but soon came back around. This time she opted for the modern one, but after some time she arrived again, her face red with frustration. Likewise, many travelers returned to this place of decision.

After some time, I saw an older man come down his path, holding the hand of a young boy with shaggy hair and curious eyes. When they came to the choice, the man knelt beside the boy and spoke quietly in his ear, pointing at all the doors as though he knew their tale. With a wise finger, he gestured to the old door so few even considered. The boy leaned in, consuming his counsel, his eyes growing bright at the old man's words.

Finally the old man straightened and seemed to leave the decision to the boy at this side. Without pause, the boy jaunted up to the old door and raised the latch. He pushed his boyish weight against it and it slowly creaked open. They passed through together, hand in hand, the opening just wide enough for the man and the boy.

And I did not see them again.

XXIX

You can't carry your twisted, poisonous thoughts into the Father's rest.

You can try but you'll just circle outside, double-minded about what you really want, trying to breathe but choking on lies.

You have to leave them behind, so that His pure perspective becomes the holy condition of your heart, making you newly equipped to live well, with full breaths of truth in your lungs.

XXX

Our most important relationships are with people who have more allegiance to our identity than to our excuses.

XXXI

Chaos is an indication of insufficient relationship. It reveals where order was achieved through control, not honor.

XXXII

The art of coercing people to respond has become big business. Companies and causes pour a lot of money into compelling us (and manipulating us) to open our wallets and our opinions, to the decision they have carefully designed.

Unfortunately, we have become so accustomed
to being lured
to being marketed to,
being shouted at from every angle,
that a response driven by identity is no longer our first instinct.

We have become lethargic, waiting for someone to make us care.

Our response mechanism--
the decision to call ourselves into action--
must not be for sale.

The response of the sons is the response of the Lord. It must be organically compelled and purely motivated.

Don't make us--your family and the earth that needs you-- beg for your response. Don't ask us buy your motivation. Don't ask us to treat His house like a marketplace.

Respond. Not because we have paid you to, but because your response is how Jesus walks the earth--or doesn't.

XXXIII
TRAIN OUT OF LIMBO

I am in limbo.

It's the nicest kind of limbo, suspended in a sort of spiritual quagmire, but without the fruitless wresting for escape. There's a voice somewhere in a muted distance, sometimes ragged and forceful, that shouts that I should impose upon myself some sort of disciplined effort of escape. But the voice has no authority, no teeth. I hear it, but pleasantly, blurred behind all my other voices.

To struggle here would be to sink deeper. To fret against this place, to wage war against this purgatory, will only further entrap me.

So I wait. Purposefully at peace.

My spirit knows to bide its time here. I am at a train station, simply waiting for the right one.

I know I have been missing from the front lines. Those whom my life is built around—I wonder what they think. Do I appear to be lazily sitting on the bench? Do they have any revelation of the divine purpose for my blurred state? Is there still honor in their hearts toward me, or is my inability to move potently in their midst planting doubt among the harvesters?

I fret in the mystery of all that is unspoken towards me.

I worry that my process would damage others. I worry that my season in this place will disqualify me to be among all those I long for. Those who will ultimately be present for my resurrection—do they have the patience to persist here in the ninth hour, in the moment when I seem a fraud?

Yet I see that my flesh assigns my deepest-feared judgments to the voices of those I love. I walk around scourged with what I believed they must be thinking: *You're a fraud! You have disappointed me! You have been found wanting! We can do this without you!*

My broken places apply masks to their faces and permit such intimate upheaval—for the deepest damage in me is not that they would say this. That, I could bear. But that these things might exist in their hearts—my craved home—and poison my place there brings me to undoing. I am insecure—wishing I could reach out for encouragement without further incriminating myself.

Yet all those thoughts I must lay aside as dirty laundry, unfit for what is ahead. I see new robes in rich colors, folded and neatly pressed—waiting for the old to finish and fall away.

He put me to sleep, gently and with great purpose, that I be honored and made ready for the road ahead. I am always as faithful as I know how to be. I get this from my Father, who is supremely faithful and knows I crave nothing more than to be potent. In the haze of momentary impotence, new authorities are laid up within me for discovery—and for mastery. Even now, as I feel things shifting—however agonizingly slow—my heart leaps to watch His fingerprints sink deep upon my clay. I wish He would rush along and finish quickly, to preserve my reputation. But it seems the pace of this process is as important as the work itself.

For indeed, the beautiful work of the Lord is done in our humblest places. For me, one who so endeavors for excellence, to be rendered here in the heat is how I know He's working in my depths. He is in my core, restructuring, refining.

It is lifting now, slowly. I realize how very much I have missed myself. All that feels lost or missing must have been worthy price for all that is coming newly awake…

XXXIV

It wasn't me.
I wasn't there.
It wasn't my fault.
It was before my time.
It was the generation before me.
It was their fight, their prejudices, their fear.

Theirs. Not mine.
The shrug of an orphan,

blind to her legacy,
blind to her inheritance.

It is up to me.
I am here now.
It is mine to repent and repair.
I was born for this time.
My generation will build and walk a mighty bridge.

This is our victory,
our compassion,
our love.

Ours. Together.
The roar of the sons of honor
in whom love overcomes,

reconciling the past with the future.

XXXV

The Lord validates who we are.
It is for Him to build and secure us.

But as members of His family,
it is upon us to communicate
the effect of each person among us,
as we experience them.

A culture of honor
consistently,
affectionately,
and boldly communicates
how its members affect one another—
not by the role they fill,
but by how our heart responds
when they are in the room.

When I see you, I feel so creative.
Something about you calls me upwards.
Everything you touch is special.
Your courage makes me walk bravely.
When you're around, I relax instantly.
Something about your voice is so comforting.
I believe in myself because of you.
Your life has helped me see through my own excuses.
When you hug me, I feel home.
I know I'm in your heart.

Their effect on my heart
is worthy of generous response.

When I offer that to them,
with clarity and gratitude,
it builds a culture of family honor.

People who honor one another
quantify the specific value of their unique presence.

XXXVI

It never fails that when I talk to my Father about something
I want, the first step is always to trust Him deeper. Every
time, He answers my heart by walking me directly through
a deep-seated insecurity.

"Until I am your roots and rest in this spot, you're going to
stay stuck, my dear. But I know you completely and I am
ready to walk with you to heal this spot. I remember why it
broke. I am the justice for that crime. I am the mercy for that
judgment. I am the grace for the recovery. I am proud that
you have reopened yourself to hope. Ah, that courage is in
My very heart! Your trust compels My deep affection for
you. Look at it through Me. Beautiful, isn't it?"

And He's right. It really is beautiful. I admire Him for how
perfectly He loves me... He knows exactly how to love me.
Of course He does; He loves me with perfect accuracy and
devotion.

Insecurity evaporates by the way He loves.

XXXVII

A house tucked in the middle of rolling acres. There, just between the yellow hills of wheat and towering corn, is a sprawling home with wide windows and an open front door.

Delicious aromas tempt you inside. An endless family table is being spread with all sorts of enticing dishes. Nourishing staples and eye-catching treats are piled high.

There is a seat for each person. You see the family gather from the far corners of the fields, from every floor of that big house. Chairs scrape the floor as each person is seated. Those coming from hard work drain their water glasses and instantly, the glass refills. The young ones are coaxed to eat their vegetables before their desserts, and their little noses wrinkle when wisdom tastes bitter. The air is filled with a mosaic hum of laughter and tears, happiness and comfort, training and rest.

From the head of the table, the Father watches it all, fully expressed by this joyful chaos. You can tell He is present, and yet partially distracted, constantly returning His gaze to an empty chair. It's the place of one of His daughters. Recently, she has struggled. He knows she is in her room upstairs, caught up in herself and fascinated by foolishness.

He aches that she has neglected her seat with Him.

He considers sending her a plate, knowing more than she of her need of it. He considers sending someone to remind her of the family and her place among them, but she already knows this well. He considers commanding her to come, but knows all too well her immature tantrums. He sends His Spirit to her and realizes that with all His persistence (and indeed, it will never cease), her casual disregard for His love had made her lazy and sullen.

A few of His close ones catch His eye and sense His thoughts. One leans close: "Papa, should I go get her?" Another reaches for the empty plate, preparing to fill it with the most delicious morsels. Who, having tasted it, could stay away? But He signals with a silent gesture, and she lowers the plate.

The sons lift their eyes to His, surprised. His eyes rim with mighty tears mixed with firm resolve.

"There is nothing more we can do," He whispers, sadness choking His words. "She will come when she is hungry."

For a time, infants are spoon-fed, but we are not babies forever. May each of us learn to take our place at the Father's table.

XXXVIII

Sonship identity is when you are able to see people with a royal conviction for all they are

with all the admiration and honor that they are absolutely worthy of

while maintaining clear sight of your own value and importance.

Any perspective of others that does not also see the fantastic puzzle piece you bring is not the sight of the Father. It is fueled by the thief of your flesh, and it results in discouragement, complacency and fruitlessness.

Sons dwell in Jesus and view all things, including themselves, in His whole context.

Sons know without question that they are uniquely and vitally important to the whole.

One identity does not trump another. They are meant to function together, one laid down for the other, submitted to one another, completing one another.

XXXIX

Sometimes the bread you think you need is the stone your good Father refuses to feed you.

XL

I told her the truth. I said what I should have said six months ago. I was honest.

She responded today and so was she. Honest. So much so that I have read it over and over, just for the privilege of reading something so clearly unveiled.

Truth in love, both love for who we each are and for who the other is.

Too much in love to lie. Too much in love to omit what was hers to know.

Truth given in purity, trusting each other to read through a heart of love. Trusting her to experience and handle whatever emotions needed handling. Trusting that if the truth broke something, the love that came with it would walk us through healing. Truth that compelled the actual experience of Jesus between us.

Truth in love is not easy. But it compels us to grow out of childishness and places a demand upon our maturity. It builds intimacy and unity, even in disagreement, because we have common love and respect and trust in free flow, even when perspectives are at odds.

You cannot have an open heart and lie. Lies are walls.

Tell the truth. Tell it bravely, awkwardly, gently, even nervously, but wrap it up with your whole heart of His love, and give it like the gift that it is.

XLI

Ok, real talk.

At some point in my late teens, someone said I was annoying.

It was one of those perfectly-timed zingers, stated by someone I respected, that went deeper than was intended. They were teasing, but they didn't know how open my heart was to them (and how seriously my teenage heart took things).

I was wounded.

I should have talked about it then, but I didn't understand how important it was to open my heart. The thorn embedded in me and impacted many of my behaviors in relating to others.

I don't think of this much. Honestly, it was years ago. But recently, I recognized a pattern. It popped up every time I wanted to express myself dramatically or honestly...every time I wanted to push back with a question that would force an issue or belabor a conversation.

"What if they think I'm annoying?"

It was crippling.

I was at a crossroads. My heart wanted to be herself, and the ghost of an old memory flinched as though a blow of rejection was imminent.

But love...

...Is bigger.

I have been loved. I have experienced it with my Father, my husband, my family, and all those who have taken me into themselves. I have walked through difficult discussions where I know that people have chosen their love for me over their own rights.

Love equips faith to overcome fear.

If I say "I don't care if I'm annoying", I'm operating in my flesh. As a spiritual daughter of my Father, it is my lifelong hope to grow in favor with all; to express myself with grace and well-seasoned words. It's immature to throw myself around without a care of how I impact what I touch.

But there *must* be friction among us, to bring our identities into balance and maturity. We express the full spectrum of our Dad. We're bound to rub each other into annoyance from time to time

It's not that I don't care if I'm annoying. It's that I'm willing to be.

Let's embrace these opportunities to grow, discover and challenge one another. To run from "being annoying" for the sake of avoiding negative experiences is to miss out on incredible intimacy.

What a beautiful door for us to grow into Him and into one another.

XLII

There is a striving—a purposeful Spirited movement—that is holy and creative.

Self-discipline and faithfulness are beautiful filters through which the flesh cannot pass.

When the flesh goes, healing and freedom are complete.

Do not resent the work of discipline. Let it serve you.

It is a friend.

XLIII

Just dwell in Me.
Draw everything of life from Me.
Ask. I will be generous.
Seek. You'll find Me.
Knock. The door will swing open.

Seek Me single-mindedly
and all those other things

your desires, ambitions and hopes,

Wild Heart,
will be added.

Added.
After you have filled your belly with Me.

Added.
After I am the entire contingency for your life.
Added.
After You and I are entirely grafted together.

I will never use flesh to satisfy spirit.
Please don't let your cravings for lesser things
keep our connection frail and incomplete.

Fill your appetites with Me.
Trust Me to perfectly satisfy you.
I made you. I get you. I understand.
I will not delay. I am never late.

Just dwell in Me.
Not partially.

Completely.

LXIV

Recently we were praying at the dinner table. Dax prayed about each of us like he always does, and when it was my turn, he said, "Thank you that Mama makes yummy food, and that she always reminds us to turn our hearts."

I was a puddle, obviously.

I often plead with them, quietly in their ears, to turn their hearts when they face the desire to be selfish, rebellious or separated. It is one of my deepest hopes in parenting them into Papa's fullness for them: that they be well-practiced in disciplining their hearts towards the way of Jesus.

Tonight we are watching *The Bible*. Over and over again we see examples of hard hearts missing out of God's perfect goodness and mercy. And again, I think Dax summarized it beautifully:

"When you don't turn your heart, it makes your heart hard, not squishy."

So there it is.

XLV

If you find yourself saying *no* more than *yes*;

If you find yourself recycling the same wounds, the same lessons, the same struggles, over and over;

If your search for the conviction of your identity seems to constantly sit just outside your reach;

Beloved, it is time to put down your fear of failure, your fear of weakness.

It is time to stand up and walk and try and fail and trust.

It is time to take the theories of your heart classroom out into the light. It is time to bank on His grace, drawing on His divine enablement.

Count on a new kind of hard.

Count on pain you haven't encountered.

Count on coming face-to-face with your worst fears.

But these pale in comparison to your heart pounding inside of you at the new opportunities you will see.

The sudden, strong way in which you feel able to do the things you so hoped you might.

The way His eyes look at you.

The way you feel His heart burst in pride over you.

You are no longer a theory, an idea that He had. In walking, you make His dream of you come alive.

XLVI
PRAIRIE FIRE

During months of difficulty several years ago,
Jesus brought me to a place in my imagination that became
very real to me.

I knew it as a wide sky of eternal twilight
just after the sun evaporates behind the mountains,
a purple sky freckled with stars.

I could go there anytime.

There was a calm sea of waving grass,
low rolling hills by a private cove
where I would meet with Him.

In my heart, this was a place of faithfulness,
a place where I could lean my spirit into His.

He was always there,

waiting, available,
ready to talk with me.

Ready to listen and be my friend.
Ready to open for me His innermost.

Today I didn't mean to go to that place,
but I closed my eyes and there it was.
Dad's and my oasis.

But it was unrecognizable.

I looked where grass should have cushioned my feet
and it was black.

No grass, no growth of any kind, not even ash.
Cracked and barren with hot redness in the gashes.

This place of my deepest intimacy had been slain to
wasteland.

He had burned it.

He had taken what was consecrated to me
and set fire.

Except He was still here,
(I could sense Him),
there was no comfort, no beauty left.
Only a earth so torched that it still glowed beneath.

I wept for a moment.
I looked around and mourned to see this precious place

destroyed.
Such violence could not be love.
I felt betrayed.

I looked for Him and found Him easily,
sensing His quietness over my shoulder.
My Rock, my Friend,

the Fire-Kindler.

I didn't ask any questions. I didn't need to.
I knew what this was.
The heaviness of mourning lay in my chest,
the necessary medallion of suffering
from what Love must do when it's time to burn the prairie.

He took my hand and we stood there,
silent and together,
entirely at peace.

Wisdom had struck the match.

The fire would redeem a great many things that my eye had
missed.

There were parasites, thorns and weeds
sneaking a living,
hiding and skimming and stealing.
Brown grass strands in the green,
signaling the quiet hints of coming decay.
There were expired things
mixed foolishly with young courage,
old cynicism stealing vigor from the field.

Be the fire hot enough, death will surrender.

A wide countryside of verdant growth was dormant
just beneath,
waiting for fire to pave aside a new spring.

He loves this place as much as I.
He burned it to show

just how much He loves me.

Fire is my friend.
The black earth will absorb tomorrow's sun.
New things will crack open

unfurl their leaves,

and push deep.

Soon, these rolling hills

will frame His precious face
not with soot, but with green.
She's a prairie, wild and at rest,
Black today
but only today.

Tomorrow brings the green and the purple.
He burned because He knows how bright her colors will be.

XLVII

Awkward is your friend.
He is a non-negotiable,
unavoidable
piece of your becoming.

Welcome him to you.
Give him a seat beside you.

Bid him to stay.
Embrace his squirming void in your belly.

Awkward will meet you
where you are growing.
If you allow him,
he will become a signal of opportunity.

Let his presence be a reminder
to no longer source this moment
and its result
by your flesh,

but by the Spirit.

XLVIII

There is a relationship in my life right now that I have to turn over to the Father every time it crosses my mind. Over and over again, far more times than I could possibly count, I walk through each day muttering: "Father, I need to see You here. I do not understand. I don't see truth here. Renew my mind!"

And while hurt and frustration are producing pain, I know better than to pass the blame.

I know the war is within.

Every time I think of this connection, my mind swirls into an angry, defensive monologue, reacting to my hurting heart. As though I've been accused when I have not. And if I force my mind to be still, I quickly see a field of weeds that shot up in seconds—lies determined to warp the truth to prove their case. To neutralize me.

I am wrestling with myself. An old way of thinking, that I have been longing to shed for years, is reluctantly starving.

But yet, it is going! It is finally losing its grip!

This is a worthwhile moment and not to be avoided or rushed, no matter how disorienting and painful it seems. If I keep my heart fixed on the eyes of my Father, it becomes so easy to finish burning in this place. I see His love faithfully proving His quality. I see His goodness in being faithful to complete what He began in me. I see His gentleness, peeling tenderly as I whimper. The heart bleeds in the spirit, too.

He is good. We can trust Him. Even when He is peeling things away, we can stay steady in our hope that He finishes all things well—including us.

XLIX

We are destroying and pulling down speculations, and deductions, and every lofty thing raised up against the knowledge of God, and we are taking every thought and perception captive to the obedience and submission of Christ... (2 Cor. 10:5)

What do you know about Jesus? Who is He?
What do you know about you? Who are you?
What do you know about us? Who are we?

There is an increasing need for each of us to stand firmly in our identities and our faith in one another, stubbornly affixed to the truth of one another against every lie, every accusation and every broken thought pattern.

Stand firm.
Do not move.

Your identity will be proven here, revealed as the genuine glory of the Father in you—in us—as you watch it bear the weight of a son or daughter against the lies that are flying around inside.

This is the time to walk counter to any spiritual poverty you feel. Examine your heart. Lay it before the Father and give Him full access to scrub away the poisons that have taken residence. He will bring your heart into repentance of all the places where you—His son or daughter—have allowed lies to neutralize your identity.

This is the posture by which we establish victorious rule of all that Jesus has overcome.

Stand firm in who you are. Do not be moved. If you have moved, repent. If you hear more lies than truth, dig deeper into the faith of Jesus

Inferiority: Burn up in the faith of His sons.
Insecurity: You hide in flesh. The Spirit overcomes you!
Anger: Dissolve in repentance.
Exclusion and isolation: Our identities cannot submit to you.
Pride: We choose to walk in the model of Jesus the servant.

The sons of God do not submit to lies.

Come out, come out, wherever you are.

L
HIS DREAM COME ALIVE

There is no greater ambition than to become.
To become whole and really alive.

To become one with the body.
To become fully active in our identity.
To be truly with Him.

Yet there remains among us a persistent hurdle to leave
behind: We must reject any obsession with our own process.

Our tendency to study with such zeal our own features is
akin to staring into a mirror. It is one angle of an
extraordinary creation, but to fully appreciate the depth and
power of what lives within us, there are more dimensions to
experience.

I wonder if fear still holds sway among us, cleverly disguised
in an illusion of sonship that is pretty but powerless?

Even though we have been lovingly and repeatedly
reminded that we are worthy, enough, able, beautiful,
powerful, free, it remains a seed, a theory, until we step out
to experience it. Until we flex the muscles of beloved sons,
we have no concept of what could be accomplished if we
only dared to move.

When we become distracted and consumed by the swirling
vortex of our internal dialogue, our gaze slips from His
example. We forget that there is nothing outside Jesus'
power and resources to accomplish. We never see Jesus
saying He was too tired, too poor, unqualified, too weak, or

insufficient. We never hear Him say that we ask for too much. We forget that the same power that raised Jesus from death is also present in us.

Jesus, thank you for showing us that it can be done.

The example of how Jesus lived is the foundation of our becoming, and is the highest possible standard we could aspire to. In reading this (and believe me, in writing it too!), are we not already intensely aware of our shortcomings? Afraid of the standard? Tempted to prefer a lesser reality of ourselves?

To rise to His standard seems impossible.

And yet, it calls to me. The power of our Father stirs in our depths. Our DNA knows who we are.

Paul was in this spot too, I think. Why else would he so clearly remind us that our weakness calls forth our Father's power?

Think about that. This suggests that in many, many places, Jesus moved without hesitation while overcoming a sense of weakness. And in His willingness, such glory and power of the Father is brilliantly and consistently displayed even today. *I do nothing of my own initiative….what I see my Father do, that I do…*

Each of us was created with this divine heritage inside. We have a purpose. We long to participate. We long to play our part.

And yet, how to begin? We know that we will fail often, and so, in moments when we might recognize an opportunity to step out, we return instead to theory. We hide, thinking that more internal processing will yield readiness. This is a pause button we have pressed for far too long: that as long as we stay in the classroom, failure is avoidable.

As long as we remain obsessed with our process, we rob the earth of the true manifestation of His heart. This is the truth we long to negotiate: weakness is an unavoidable feature of becoming.

There is nothing wrong with ongoing instruction from our precious Jesus. In fact, He is the living food we are made to live from—endless heart-to-heart conversation with Him. This continued dialogue is vital. We can never forget that He is real. Alive. He is the person who transfers our fascination from theory to His living revelation. This intimate place of rest invites us into His perspective.

We do a dreadful thing to devalue His vision of us.

Who am I? is not the question we were made to ask. It is the position we were made to live from. While asking it is necessary in our becoming—and in our healing—it should eventually become the invisible foundation of our house upon which a new question causes fruit to burst forth: *Father, what do we see now? What are You doing?*

And then, upon Him in this true identity–a breathing structure rises upon an unshakable root, bringing provision, hope, and healing.

Forward is the fruit of identity.

LI-LXXV

LI

Last night, in an jovial error of judgment, Nick and I started making all sorts of dog barks while loading the kids into the van: high pitched yelps, deep woofs and howls.

The kids soon caught on and for a dreadful century the car sounded like a kennel, until finally the game was worn out. Nick brought the noise to a close with a firm: "OK, all the dogs fell asleep. No more dog noises."

For a moment, there was festive silence.

And then, from a mischievous dark corner of our friendly van came: "Mooooooo!"

LII
POUR OUT YOUR HEART

Trust in Him at all times, O people;
Pour out your heart before Him;
God is a refuge for us. Selah. (Psalm 62:8)

I was with David up to this point. But I couldn't figure out why he strung these phrases together. Why would he tuck in the advice "Pour out your heart before Him"? At best, it felt random.

David was an intentional writer. He did not merely collect a series of buzz words in a poem to make himself feel better. No, David was purposeful.

So I paused, stumped. Why here "Pour out your heart"? Why in the middle of an ode to God's refuge and strength is there a sudden emphasis on pouring out my heart?

Then I saw the "Selah." Even David knew I'd need a moment.

And then it came...almost audibly: "What happens when you pour out your heart to Me?"

And I imagined this gushing torrent of all my insides: my good beautiful things, my broken reality, my anger, worry, bitterness, fear...all pouring out of me.

Leaving behind in my heart an empty openness.

Pouring my heart out to my Father is what makes room for His perspective. When I heave forth exactly what I'm thinking and feeling, I empty any hidden lies of their power.

I have literally laid ashes before Him and opened the way for beauty.

The original translation for *refuge* is "protection from storms and danger." But also—get this—"protection from falsehood."

Pouring everything out and laying it all transparently before His gaze makes falsehoods immediately and completely apparent. Held inside and unchallenged by Love, they breed and spread, contaminating our hope.

It is time to pour out our hearts before Him. Not just a nearby friend, a spiritual guide or a convenient connection, though those can be good.

No. It's time to go into the backyard, the car or the shower and pour it all out before Him.

Watch! You will find His refuge for you is not a cold Bible verse tucked in a Psalm, but a warm and honest place that has always been waiting for you.

Go, now. The Father is waiting.

LIII

Where outside circumstances cause negative turmoil in me, I can identify what of me is not yet sourced by Jesus.
This is a beautiful opportunity.

LIV
DISILLUSIONED

For several years now, our family has been part of a community that has practiced with each other—In every sense of the word—what it means to be God's family; what it means to be home with the Father in our spirits as well as home with one another; figuring out what it means to really have open hearts.

And I celebrate every advancement we have gained, because He is so good and so full and rich. He's the whole point. What He has done with our beginnings is miraculous—akin to changing water into wine. We are His glory in every sense.

But we are practicing and learning, and we're always in some state of progress, allowing the Father's ideas about love and family to override our imperfect biases and broken experiences. We're rough sometimes. We're not always good at what we say we're after, and we all have blind spots. We have identities that are being exhumed and insecurities that take time to walk away from.

It's painfully clear that we're practicing and are not yet in mastery of what we see He's after. Our flaws show. And that's OK. It has to be that way. His grace is made for these gaps, and frankly, His strength shines in these places. Our imperfect is the showcase for His perfect.

But sometimes…*sigh.*

Sometimes our shortcomings in being family together are more painful—less palatable—than we've had to endure before, and it hurts more than we ever expected. Love always does. The ideal meets the playing field and scores as many fouls as points.

It can be tough to remember to cover one another in love when we feel victimized by a lack of it. We face disappointment and are brought to the pressure points that up until now we have carefully avoided. Typically, these things include a need for confrontation, a feeling of rejection, or other relational crimes…things we formerly felt the freedom to subtly distance ourselves from.

When we encounter these things in other areas of our lives, we complain…and just casually stop engaging.

But in the family culture, engagement is everything. We know we shouldn't "leave" (meaning: tune out)—and truly, we don't mean to. We also feel clueless on how to bridge the gap we're facing (and the gap, unaddressed, becomes distance.)

We're in pain—or we're confused—or we're angry—and we stand there, sort of at a loss on what to do next. We don't know how to "holy it up" to say it right. We don't want to come off rude. Sometimes a wall goes up, purely by instinct. We judge, we mope, or we click into survival mode in the very place where we are called to thrive.

Forward progress stops.

In some cases, the hard work of practicing family has left some of us with unforgiven disappointment that has begun to transition into disillusionment.

This disillusionment—a hopeless, guarded cynicism about something you previously found valuable—is dangerous to our heart and identity. It will fuel distance, empower victimized thinking, validate gossip and—most tragic—allow us to justify a domino-effect of unjust offenses or poor decisions. It will steal our freedom and make it very hard to hear the Father accurately.

In this place, faith starves to death.

This is completely avoidable, and un-ironically, family is the solution. But we will have to be willing to step out on the water, and allow family to be what we have not yet trusted it to be.

We need to open up and say what's going on inside. When we say "open up," we mean it. We know it won't always sound good, be eloquent or even make sense. Choose your moment, your audience, and your spirit well. But you need to open, without attack, and lay all the poison that's been swirling around inside. Expel it. Submit yourself to us, in Him.

Remember, we're all sitting in Him together, practicing, learning, bringing each other to perfection. So to each one: You need to let it come out and trust us to meet you there.

You can't go to your room in the Father's house, behind a soundly closed door and argue that you're in the house, just not at the table. That's silly. There's a feast going on here, and you have a seat at the table.

Straight talk warning.

Hiding in your room is a form of tantrum. Eventually, mature sons have to grow out of the idea that someone should come to pry them open. You have been entrusted with every necessary ingredient of restoration. Be strong, take courage, and use them!

It is not OK to be silent in this place, at least not long term. It is good, for a time, to wisely weigh the things you're thinking and feeling and ask the Father to help you expand your love and grace for others. Freedom is maintained by forgiveness, and unselfishness will help you to see the full picture.

Ask for help to lay aside whatever expectations or fears you might have about how you're received. We probably won't validate everything you say or agree with everything you feel. If we did that, we'd be operating outside our identities, bringing temporary comfort but no lasting brotherhood.

Being your family takes as much courage for us as is does for you.

There might be a small moment or two of angst. There might be a hot word or a spat. Someone might cry or need a little time to process. But no one is going to run. No one is going to leave or give up. What's happening in you has happened, on some level, inside of us too.

Our promise to you is: If you want, we will help you climb out of this particular cave on our way up the mountain.

Pray for healing from whatever idol has been built about the idea of family. It must be torn down as we bravely begin to walk out the real heavenly Family of God.

Pray that the Father Himself wins inside each heart, that mercy and humility and unity overcome, and that peace and rest can reign in places that right now are anything but calm.

His family is strong because it is built and sustained by the person of Jesus, revealed in our practice and ever-deepening maturity. Let's give each other room, let's commit to communicate, and let's each hold our own part of things.

Our unity is worth every struggle.

LV
OPPORTUNITY

We have a broken understanding about opportunity.

It comes, and we don't capture it.
It comes, and we can't rearrange our lives to say yes.
It comes, and we fail to value it.
It comes, and it looks like work.
It comes, and it doesn't care about our reputation.
It comes, and we let it pass us by.

It comes, and it goes,
seeking those whose hunger is stronger than their fear.

Opportunity is all around us. And most of the time, taking hold of it will mean letting go of something else.

LVI
THE BREAD, THE DOOR

This morning, from the moment I started to wake up, my heart was troubled. By the time I was truly awake, I was in the weeds. I won't take you through the specifics or the long trek by which my identity restored itself, but I will offer a daughter's heart for moments like this.

We are all in different stages, as our individual sonship becomes an all-the-way-through reality by which we are unshaken in every place. When we are immature, we gauge this by how we feel at the moment. If we feel strong, our sonship is strong. If we feel bad, our sonship is weak.

It's true that our feelings are strong, purposeful, and are not to be ignored. Neglecting our emotions is not the victory of them. They are to be experienced, tested, sometimes shared, and most importantly, submitted to the reality of Jesus. In this, we are invited to align every detail of who we think we are to who He says we are.

Therein lies a shaking.

However, it is not the quake that brings forth the reality of our sonship, but our willingness to stubbornly and calmly adhere to the rock of Jesus despite how we feel. Sometimes, even that rock seems to shake, but this reveals only our own inaccuracies about Him. When we trust Him, we discover with unspeakable joy an unshakeable union with Him. Fear speaks, but love in relationship drowns it out.

We learn to relax when everything that can be shaken no longer trembles under pressure. *Greater is He who is in me...*

Do not allow familiarity to breed contempt in these simple and eternal truths that Jesus gave us. His originals are still perfectly current:

"I am the Bread of Life."

When we are in the weeds, we tend to seek strength and comfort in artificial places, much like a child who wants candy when they need meat and vegetables. In those moments, we become acutely aware that our religious structures are empty of what our heart so clearly needs. This is true–but it is not true that Jesus is empty of what we need. The shaking puts us in the position to relearn what it is to taste and see, showing us all the places we believed were food but are not.

I will never forget the day that I was so hungry and broken– and in full rebellion because I knew every place I thought to go for help wasn't going to fill me. I became depressed, believing I was alone. I wept to Jesus, angry and confused– and I encountered Jesus as Bread of Life for the first time. Him and me–in reality–in Spirit and in Truth–at the core of who I really am. That day, I sang to Him "You are my Bread of Life," and I knew what His food really was. I knew why He said man does not live by bread alone.

We don't have to climb out of the weeds. In the moment we fix our eyes on Jesus and eat of Him, we lose sight of the weeds entirely, instantly restored to our rightful position. This isn't something our flesh accomplishes; it is something our spirit remembers.

"I am the Door."

How much of our internal drama exists because we attempt to pick up the dreams inside of us before we have the spiritual maturity to carry them? We get glimpses of big things, glimmers of explosive visions and hints of how big we really are, and we latch onto those dreams instead of taking hold of Him–forgetting that Jesus is the context for everything we will ever manifest.

It is understandable to take encouragement when our hearts begin to believe that we are truly important, because the world bars no holds in accusing us of insignificance. It is undeniably soothing to hear our heart start saying *I have ideas in me! I see things! I believe that this new thing is possible!* But take care that we do not allow the revelations of the Spirit to become opportunities for the flesh.

To dive in there, before Jesus fills up what He has sketched out, is like a toddler running foolishly to the deep end of the pool, unequipped to live through the adventure he's chasing. There is an unromantic middle–the training up of the people who will carry the mission–and it is non-negotiable. The delay between the recognition of an idea and the walking out of a vision is only frustrating to the foolish. We can gauge where we are in maturity by how willing we are to trust the Father to open the right door, in the right place, at the right time, for the realization of what we hope for.

In the meantime, stay faithful and do not despise small opportunities. See them as invitations that they are, and pave open your availability to them. Make it so that the Father can say of you, as he did in Revelation 3: *He who is holy, who is true, who has the key of David, who opens and no one will shut, and who shuts and no one opens, says this: 'I know your deeds. Behold, I have put before you an open door which no one can shut, because you have a little power, and have kept My word, and have not denied My name…*

Everything we are encountering and overcoming is meant to bring us to the irreversible and unshakable Root by which we not only are convinced of His identity but of our own.

In His love, Jesus also bars no holds in His perfect commitment to bring forth in us a life that really lives Him.

LVII
CONFLICT

Conflict is important.

Really important.

I wouldn't say I love conflict, but I'm old enough now to have experienced countless times that my relationships were made deeper because we walked through conflict together.

I don't crave conflict, but I do get suspicious if I go long periods of time without encountering it among those I consider close to me. It means my connection to that person has weakened, or at best, plateaued. As one who craves for depth, it is important to me to know that those who love me are also encountering my reality.

Conflict for me is a good benchmark to know if we are continuing to truly engage one another. To me, this is peacemaking, not peacekeeping.

These conflicts are not always expressed between the two of us. Sometimes the conflict is inside of me—a valuable invitation to discover my identity, what is hiding it, and what must be expressed.

But paradoxically, I have also lost my appetite for conflict, and even more, I am easily wearied of it when it smacks of superficialities or redundancies. Love is patient and so am I, though I'll be honest enough to say that one time around any particular topic is enough for me. Twice is sometimes profitable, and three times sometimes necessary. But after that, I have trouble engaging.

Like you, I have been repeatedly flogged with expectations that are not in alignment with who I am, and those have been a struggle for me to forgive. I am not saying I have not forgiven; I am saying I have been saddened to see how slow my heart lets go, far past my will to quickly recover. So conflict is a crapshoot. It can be hugely profitable, but it may come with a need to forgive.

I cannot tell you how many times I pray for a pure and open heart. *Create in me a clean heart. I repent for what was mine. Make me so deep in grace and justice and forgiveness. Give Your love in me such courage and realness…*

All that to say this: Sons must allow conflict to expand all the way to its borders but never past them. Conflict must never be allowed to sever the loyalty and lovingkindness by which the people we love remain fully confident of our commitment to them. It must never be the scale by which we weigh out the value or honor we give them. It must never stop us worshipping and serving alongside the very people with whom we are embattled.

There are deep and high lessons that love in conflict will embroider in us.

Those of us with strong sibling relationships understand this phrase: I'm allowed to mess with you, but no one else is.

Obviously this doesn't mean we get sole rights to abuse others, but rather it's an expression that says, "I love you so much and I know you trust me. And I trust my heart about you. I'm protective of you, no matter how ugly you and me looks right now. I've got your back. I love you enough to engage you so that we keep encountering each other more deeply–and I'm not going to fake anything with you–but that doesn't mean it's me versus you. It's always going to be us together, going after what we see."

The deep bond this develops is critical to what we hope for. It starts with us being willing to allow our relationships to walk through—not around—conflict, instead of withholding truth when it's obviously going to combust. It's looking at people who conflict with us and teaching our hearts to see their friction as friendship and the fight as love-building.

Love is cut short when conflict is avoided.

Conflict rages when unity attempts to take ground. Whether or not we stand bravely and allow it to deepen us is up to us.

Better is open rebuke
Than love that is concealed.
Faithful are the wounds of a friend,
But deceitful are the kisses of an enemy. (Prov 27:5-6)

LXIII

The deepest, most perfect encounters of Jesus
are when I'm with people,

who are whole pieces of His reality.

Experiencing instead of romanticizing.
Observing instead of judging.
Absorbing instead of enduring.

Completely open,
Sponge-like and simple.

Taking whole pieces of them into me.
Taking Him into myself,
straight from their easy being into my own.

How have we made it so complicated for so long?
Look, right there He is—in you.
Look, right here He is—in me.

More real, more alive,
more right in front of our eyes,
than we ever dared hope.

LIX
THE END OF TREASON

I don't know how to begin, except that I must.

I read the words from John 15 and I cannot get away from them: *Abide*. Abide in Me.

It's been cycling in me for weeks. Months. *Abide in Me.*

It has become obvious that I am double-minded and full of hypocrisy. I still need help accepting what I have been trying not to hear: that the reality of my life falls short of what I say I'm after.

I've developed a hybrid life that seems holy but isn't. I like it because it allows to me keep all the things I don't want to overcome and lay claim to an shell-game inheritance that requires little from me. What's more: few challenge me on it because my half-life validates their own—and there we commune, teetering jovially between love and death.

Abide in Me. Unless you abide in Me, you cannot bear fruit.

Recently, some friends—beautiful Jesus lovers—shared with me a decision that cut me deep because their choices were so detrimental. And yet they were indifferent, even defensive, of their sin. Didn't they realize how expensive their callousness would be?

I raged inside, hurting and sad, until the Father's Spirit cut me wide open: *Are you so different? Abide in Me. I've been saying it to you, over and over. Abide in Me. I am Home. I am Source. I am the Bread of Life. There is no other. Abide in me!. I am the Standard--come higher!*

It's not that I've been involving my life in some terrible activity or dark secret. I don't have dusty skeletons to expose. But once the Spirit calls you out of a thing— anything—to remain is sin.

I have stayed far too long in silly things that keep me from everything I long for. I have been double-minded in my repentance, and I resent that love would constrain me. If it is really Freedom's voice, won't I like its sound?

No. Freedom's voice is always sandpaper if the son has grown sleepy.

Abide in Me. If you abide in Me, and my words abide in you, ask whatever you wish and it will be done…

But the smorgasbord of the earth is wide and glittering. An entire world system screams for my attention and lures me with entitlements and busyness. It numbs my heart and seduces the euphoric release of my opinions, fueling division and anger and belittling righteousness. The noise is designed to capture my fascinations, and I don't notice the cloying soundtrack by which the sounds of hell are disguised.

With time, their façade becomes how I think. I share their perceptions and limitations. My relationships encounter tragic wounds. I spend my money in their systems and expand their influence. I adopt their fears and false identities. I give life to something that is destined to be destroyed. I negotiate my rebellion, trying to justify a living that by definition can never be Life.

Jesus, forgive Me. I was blind, but now I see.

It's like sugar—once we are addicted, it's incredibly difficult to pry the mind free. The taste buds become numb to what real bread tastes like.

Abide in Me. Every branch that does not bear fruit, He takes away…

But this is where I am, in the purest, most unreligious way I can express. I cannot let go of the invitation…*Abide in Me! I am the Perfect Context and Fulfillment for everything that is in you. If you have appetite for someone or something you can't find in Me, look again. Look again! I am laying My chest open to you.*

It seems drastic to depart from the hypothetical, where I could still convince myself of a realm in which all things are permissible and beneficial. But I was made for kingdom life, and that appetite for treason carries the now-repellant hiss of death.

It's a little hard, sometimes, to eat "Bread" I can't touch, and "Abide" in a place I can't see. It feels unnatural to choose invisible over tangible. I think it seems hard because I have spent more of my life training my physical senses than my inward spirit. I have pursued the sugar-laced factory food long enough to gag at its smell.

Invincibly, when He becomes my Bread, things of Him just for me bubble up that are priceless and perfect and transformative. The pure fruits of the Spirit etch themselves upon my soul.

So these days I am learning to allow all my appetites to lay in front of me, examining each without loyalty. Am I commanding the stones to be made into bread?

LX

I'm not going to talk at you with what I believe. The world has had a bellyful of talk. There are words everywhere and I have grown weary of them. Empty words propping up dry bones.

But I will break open my chest and give you Who I know. I will pour Him out—the Word, the Living Water. I will bring you to Him. I will walk with You to His chest until you are buried there, entirely and irreversibly ruined for anything less than His love and reality in every part of you.

Until you feel His air in your very lungs.

LXI
A STAGE AND A SEAT

She wore a dress that cost more than my student loans.
He owns five properties free-and-clear, and I'm underwater on my
house.
They said it only costs $30 a month. Only?!

I wanted to slap someone.

I hang my shoulders, turn my pockets out and make a pitiful
face.
I feel small, and I hate feeling small.

In an effort to feel better, I think like a fool,
and I believe what I think.

I step onto a stage and deliver my speech:

Here, let me criticize your wealth.

Especially when you have more money than I do.
Somehow my poverty is holier than your success.

I detest your joy and I resent your adventures.
I fear and yet long for your freedom.
I hate how it makes me feel to see you live how I do not.
I don't see your work or the cost you paid, only thornless roses.

My heart delivers this speech blisteringly
with eloquence and cadence
like a player on a stage delivering her embittered monologue
to an audience of the destitute.
There is a weird, tarred blackness in my throat.

I continue to the finish:

Therefore, I will stand in gross judgment,
chest puffed with empty wind,
pointing a finger of ignorance and entitlement.

That you would live like I cannot offends me.

That you would make me feel like this means
you must be cruel and oppressive
and I am the defenseless victim of your success.

That you do not politely sink to the level of my comfort
infuriates me!

I give a deep bow to thunderous applause.
My defeat is delivered in indignant self-pity.

But the scene is not done.

As though a twin of myself,
I walk onto the stage from the left.
Stepping up five golden steps,
I take the elevated seat.

The applause dies down as I take my place,
facing down the warped thing that looks like me
but sounds like death.

The place is silent.
Slowly, water begins to trickle from my chest.
The seated me begins,

quietly, but without hitch.

Indeed, the voice of a queen will reset this place,
for it is buried in death and twisted in lies.

The ground trembles a little as authority secures it.
The trickle flows a little faster, and the front of my dress is
covered in light.

I call up the divine blueprint from His heart in me,
the seed that knows I am worthy, capable and purposed.

Why have I decided to malign the one I could be learning from?

When did I cease to believe in my own capacity to build, to earn,
to succeed?

When did I hold sure-things and safety closer to me than wisdom
and adventure? Have I not a Good Teacher?

Is my Father, the Might of All Creativity, so small in me,
that His inspiration is drowned by an orphan's whimper?

Does not everything of Him belong to us?

The water is flowing quickly now, down across the stage
and onto the feet of the crowd.
It rises quickly.
Everything it touches is like black mud dissolved into gold.
Skin glistens and black eyes turn to blue crystal.
Hearts pound like a drum,

and one voice becomes many,
so powerful that the walls of the theatre evaporate.
We start to echo like a wind.

Here, we see feet and hands!
We see eyes and mind and courage!

There is a great rumble.

Feet, flex and stand and climb!
Hands, pick up and lift and carry!
Eyes, see open doors!
Mind, think with wisdom, freedom and power!

Let us build the tangible and the intangible.

Let us be filled with honor for every weight.

Let us encourage and respect the bearers!

Water pours out of us all,
and we cover the earth.

Here, let us build together! The Might of All Creativity is alive.

He is in us after all!

LXII

Simply put: I don't think God cares about fairness.
Not like we do.
I don't think fairness is in His nature.

Fairness is a hollow, manmade concept
only sustained by insecurity
an entitlement that prolongs our immaturity.

The world cries for fairness
when it truly craves justice.

Fairness is an impossible construct
an unsolvable equation
that neuters identity.

Far, far better,
far, far higher,
is God's justice,
borne by the full weight of His mercy
and backed by His sovereign design.

Fairness cares about feelings;
justice cares about identity.

Fairness prioritizes equal results;
justice champions equal value.

Fairness is fueled by wounds;
justice is fueled by love.

Fairness and justice are not the same.
Fairness is counterfeit justice.

Justice is in the bedrock of any courageous society.

LXIII

Tonight Nick was reading to the kids from *The Lion, the Witch and the Wardrobe*. Dax interrupted, asking if the story was real, and Aly answered him very seriously, explaining to his curious eyes that it was fiction. There couldn't really be magic doors and talking beavers.

Nick and I paused right there and asked her: "Why not?"

I said, "I think that as we become more and more like Jesus, and the earth returns to its origin, we might get to talk to the animals! I think it would be so fun to understand them. We'll walk around with them in shining authority, as friends!"

She was taken aback and we loved that moment when her the simple faith of her childhood—the Jesus magic of her childlike heart—was contended for. You could almost see the pilot light in her magical heart flare blue with fire. Dax's eyes danced with adventure. Imagine the day when he might race a cheetah!

I know that's maybe a little nuts, but it's just what I hope for. I want everything to be just like our Father originally made it--maybe even getting to walk beside a lion with my fingers in its mane.

Tomorrow I will tell them the stories of Philip who was caught up in the Spirit and taken away. Of Elijah who went to the Father in a fiery chariot. Of Jesus, who appeared despite a locked door.

They are not merely stories. They are reality. For me, they are encouragement for the age we will see and experience. Yes, even greater things are laid before us.

We cannot allow the dull fade of false truth to silently steal away the inherent faith in children. The power of their Christlike faith will equip these kids to rise up in leadership of the earth we are restoring. Yes, let maturity and sonship be prepared in them, but let it never be at the expense of the perfect purity.

I refuse. I tell you, I refuse. As their mother, I am called to contend for the priceless purity and vision of my children; to measure what we teach them against the example of Christ.

Let us have the courage to make Jesus' reality the world we present to our children. And align our own world to Jesus who roars in our depths.

LXIV

To walk deliberately out of an old way of thinking into a
new one is awkward for me.
I'm terrible at the new way.
I mean it. I require a lot of longsuffering.

Nothing about it feels right or familiar or even good.

I remember and re-encounter all the chicken exits.
I take steps and I wrestle with every inch.
I stand steady under scrutiny, burning inside.
I stumble around without dignity.
I feel conspicuous and embarrassed.

I hate the new way.

Steady, dear heart.
The expectation is not perfection—the Standard is.
And in Him is the grace for all your practice.

So Spirit, fill me with the thoughts of my Father.
Renew my mind
so that my heart chooses the new, hard way
over and over again.
So that failure doesn't persuade me to fear.

Love, sustain me. Renew me.

Until the real me overcomes in You.

LXV

We can get upset and discouraged
about what people don't understand about us,
starving for all that feels withheld from us.

Or we can live
and provide opportunity to be discovered all over again.

One is bondage and death and fear-of-man,
another lap in that nauseating wilderness.

And one is freedom and family and life,
chest open wide to immortality.

The hang-ups are prison bars for the new man inside. Don't
go there because you think it's where others want you. No!
Keep going, keep revealing, keep expanding.

I promise, we'll catch on. We'll see. Don't let our initial
confusion, surprise, lack of response, or even skepticism
frustrate you. We don't mean to be discouraging. We are
cute but slow sometimes.

If it takes us a minute, be patient with us. Walk with clear
eyes and a strong heart. Love us. Be consistent and brave.

Be alive among us. Walk in freedom and service by the
Spirit.

Jesus will faithfully cause the newness of you, and Him in
you, to overwrite everything we used to think we knew.

LXVI

To be "empowered,"
to be commissioned and endowed
with real authority and freedom,
is the result of mutual covenant.

The one with resource and authority commits to pouring
out, and the one with ability and passion treats that
wellspring with right value.

Empowerment always partners with hunger. Always.

The best of any father is reserved
for those of genuine passion.

Authority and empowerment is seated
on the throne of a father
and is only released to truly-invested sons.

If we sit and wait for empowerment to find us,
demanding it thread the needle of our fragmented attention,
wanting it to meet our limited availability,
or forcing it to take a form most convenient for us,

we demonstrate entitlement,

a heart incapable of fostering a father's seed,
a heart incapable of empowerment,
a heart too blind for inheritance.

Entitlement is death to sonship.

There is no empowerment without sonship.
There is no empowerment without hunger.

LXVII

As my children get older, my primary role is evolving.
Lately, my heart is required to contend for our family to
learn to listen.

Listen to their daddy. Full stop.

Listen to me. Full stop.

Listen to each other, vigilantly maintaining our family codes
for honor, trust and teamwork.

Listen and turn themselves toward good advice without
pulling birth order rank or hiding behind a lie.

Listen to the spirit of a thing.

The more I plead for them to listen,
the higher the standard becomes for me.

Listening to their daddy.
Listening to them.
Listening to wisdom.
Listening to the Spirit.
Listening to you.

I feel we could all listen
a little bit more than we are now.

I wonder how our intimacy would deepen
if we gently made sure
that those who speak
are heard.

LXVIII
WILD REST

Daughter,
there is no rest for you in your emotions.

They cannot be for you what I am.

They are a merciless, endless parade of reactions,
incompatible with freedom.

One minute you're up, the next, you're low.

Emotions used as a compass build only a cyclone.

In a rare, clear moment, a scene plays in your mind:
You see yourself astride a carved saddle
in a carousel of horses weaving
up and down
their painted garish faces devoid of breath,
steel rods through their spines.
Around and around and around you go,
high and low
tossed
the canned song piercing your vibrant blueprint
repeating
coercing reactions
and driving you mad.

Oh beloved, do you hear My heart aching that you would be
brave, that you would take one look into Me and trust Me
completely?
Trust Me forever?

Don't trust how you feel if it conflicts with My character and love.
For I have laid before you endless acres of territory…

There is within you the invitation.

Just outside the carousel gate, awaiting.
He is magnificent

lungs heaving
adventure pulsing from His nostrils.

You bite your lip: Do you dare?

Almost by impulse, you slip down from the puppet pony,
leap the fence in four strides
and climb upon the broad-shouldered steed, bareback.

And you let Him have His head.
Is that the mane of a horse or a Lion?

He carries you through wind and clouds, over hills and
valleys, your hair flying behind you. The tin chime of the
old way fades as He puts miles between you and your
impostor life.

You feel His heartbeat radiating through your womb, and
real femininity forms in your spirit. You become truly
beautiful, almost other-worldly, sourced from living bread
and water. You glide as one, no longer gripping His mane
in fear.

All around you see the perimeter of black storm.

But it cannot touch you. It tries, with long jointed fingers
that reach into your very soul. It grabs and threatens and
shakes.
But not even the gates of hell have power against you.

You laugh. He laughs. *...and she laughs without fear of the future...*

This is the true rest, the rooted life of Jesus. It is freely available, and yet so few risk it.

Why does the carousel feel so safe, Wild One?

Come out into the wild with Me, lest the carousel lull you into tormented sleep. Let Me light you up.

Venture out into the brave Truth of all He is.

From this place, there is resource, strength and courage for every moment. There is freedom from the aching, endless mental wheel.

There is clarity to see the crouching snakes coiled behind each shadow, their bellies full of dust.

Ah, yes, serpent. You have spoken before. Your face of dust reveals your eternal sentence. I have no time for you.

Rise up, daughter of the Lord. Strap courage across your breasts and stare down all that you once feared.

Do you feel the gold rising up from deep within? Let it fund you with strong faith, and give it your voice, your feet, your heart.

Withhold nothing. Do not shrink back. Do not posture command or demand. Do not overthink. Simply dwell and move in the absolute confidence that He is, and that you are in Him.

Oh, beloved, I see you. Do you see the sweat on My brow, My labored breath?

I have been pursuing you.
I have ached that you would say My name, take My name, and
tuck yourself entirely within Me.

Rest, Daughter.

Bring all that you feel into submission to His narrow way
and freeing truth. Turn your carousel mind to His simple
perspective and allow complexity to reveal its foolishness.
Rest into that great big chest and breathe free—
you are,
and have always been,
cradled wildly there—at Home.

LXIX

Trembling shaking
Silently bursting
Quietly yearning
Words completely inadequate.
Belly burning
Heart weeping
Entirely undone and choked at the sight of this glory.
There is no composure for this favored heart.
Humming the sounds of a once far-off shore
now so close.
I cannot un-see what I have seen.

LXX

The building of relationships in the Father's precious family is a keystone piece of His culture.

And yet...it's a *thing*. Schedules, hosting, meals, planning, money, cleaning, exhaustion, babysitters, kids, time...

Are we making it too hard?

What if these expectations and pressures have actually contaminated the life of the Family? What if these are the world's factories of obsolete thinking? What if we are really free of those confines?

If we welcomed people into time with the real me, exactly as we are, would we discover the hidden gems of real community and family that the Father had in mind? Would we rediscover an original design that completely disarms and transcends fear?

We are terrible at being anyone other than us. It's exhausting, discouraging and empty. But the real us--now that is a river of life.

What if you walked into my house and I handed you a basket of laundry to fold? What if I fed you leftovers for lunch or just scrambled some eggs for dinner? What if instead of chattering, we let the moment hang there until something real and beautiful rose from the deep? What if our family came over and we worked on a list of chores you never have time to do? What if you didn't clean up before I came? What if I didn't cancel for a headache and you came just to watch Gilmore Girls with me?

Do we heal one another when our love is honest? When we meet together in honor and with fascination, does family naturally result?

What if identity began to set the culture of our homes and our interactions, and we learned to seek one another with genuine, tangible curiosity?

Would we become endeared to the amazing, weird, original people we discover? Would insecurity be eradicated from among us?

LXXI

Lately my spirit has been wandering into uncharted territory with the Father. I have all these ideas about Him that I've never heard before.

You'd think that wondering into the unknown, away from Main Street and off the map, would cause me to feel insecure.

But it's entirely the opposite. The further we go, the more secure in Him I become, even though some areas of this journey could, with time, directly contradict my former convictions.

As I loaded the dishwasher this morning, I began to marvel at this, that the Father and I could travel away from the shore together. I realized how weird it was that I had allowed questions to come to traditional areas of my theology without triggering my lifelong alarms of caution.

I was walking on water with no fear of sinking.

This is how we know we are actually rooted in a person and not a belief system. We stop protecting the laws of our belief structure, and are no longer made secure by a manmade script. We relax into a Spirit-born life that can freely explore the vast expanse within Him, knowing that if we misunderstand, He is the perfect Teacher and Father, perfectly able to perfectly redirect us.

This is loving Him with all our mind—prizing Him above every other conviction, opinion and speculation.

I have found that when I trust in my structures, I feel insecure when they are challenged. But oh—when I trust Him, I am perfectly secure no matter how shaky He proves my old mindsets to be.

LXXII

Today while Thijs napped, Dax shoved his feet into his work boots, tossed on a hoodie and joined me in the rain. We tackled a bramble of old overgrown bushes beside our house, preparing to pull them out. We pruned, pulled and grunted, and the brush pile grew high.

He stood nearby as I worked on a particularly thick branch. I noticed how weak some of the roots had become, and we enjoyed forcing them loose. Then I saw how some obnoxious vines had twisted themselves in the underbrush and before I knew it, I was talking to them.

"You cannot grow here," I said quietly as I wrestled them loose. "Beauty, I call you from this soil. This is my land. Weeds, you cannot grow here. The curse is finished. Life: Spring forth."

Dax heard me. "Mommy, why are you talking to the roots?"

"Because Jesus gave us the earth, Dax," I said. "Because Jesus destroyed everything that the devil did. Because it's ours, and we get to bless and curse. This is our land, and Mommy is calling it alive."

Dax didn't question. "Oh, OK."

This is the new normal, the return to the beginning. I love that Dax will remember his mother talking to the earth. I love that in modeling Jesus, the rising generation will walk with us into His increase, of which there is no end. I love our genius Father. I see Him increasing in every place.

LXXIII
CYCLE OF SABOTAGE

I hadn't really ever noticed it before, but now it was really starting to bug me. I looked at the text in my hand, and saw how she had phrased it. I laid my phone down and pulled out of the parking lot, still puzzled by what I suddenly wanted to say and how strong it was.

I waited at the red light, turn signal blinking. I knew I was hearing the Father, and I knew I needed to say something.

But as I considered a response to my friend, I saw a major hurdle in my own life—a roadblock I had always felt but never explored.

In the past, when I saw something in the life of another that concerned me,

something that love itched to speak to,

I would freeze.

Spirals of insecurity would start twisting inside of me. I would stew for weeks. I was immobilized by fear that I would get it wrong. Sometimes I would go to others with my concern, trying to validate myself by building a mental army of mutual opinion.

Before I had begun, I was convinced it would end poorly, the first person in history for which His grace was too small. *Eyeroll.*

Sometimes I was too full of judgment to see the root with compassion, too caught up in the storm of their life to see the fragile part of them that needed me.

In these moments, I was offered a partnership with the Spirit to pour powerful love into the life of another, and my flesh blinded me.

There was a time when a delay between my impulses and my actions was necessary. I had a sharp tongue and an arrogant heart, and when I tried to merge them with my identity, there was a crash. So for a time, my patient Father trained me with silence and fire and terrible inner combat.

He faithfully resurrected me, trained me in humility and compassion, and most importantly, taught me to love people. The time came to try again and I flinched, afraid to hurt people I now loved. The risk seemed too great.

My heart was now soft but the walk of love was incomplete, lacking the fruit that practice would bring to it.

This cycle has sabotaged my identity a million times. I have swallowed my tongue, choking on manna that spoiled because I did not serve it. It soured in my belly, stealing from me what it would have provided to another.

When you truly love someone with the Father's heart, love makes way for the thing you need to say. Grace meets you there. Holy Spirit Himself does the work.

But because I knew the storm of struggle such encounters have sometimes caused in me, I wanted to spare others that process, or at the very least, I did not want to be the instigator. I avoided dealing in the Love that has transformed me. Love has been most faithful to me when it did not spare the pain I needed to walk through.

So here I sat at the red light, suddenly seeing the wall I kept investing in. I knew Love well enough, and trusted my own heart enough, to see myself at the roadblock. I could turn to the side, ponder this thing longer, stew over it with frustration and angst, push it to the side of my mind and ignore it with any number of the distraction techniques I have mastered.

Or I could look straight ahead, into and through the eyes of my Father and ask, Why is this coming to me now, and what is in my heart to do with it?

Imagine letting our Author help us turn the page.

The light turned green and I hit the gas, turning right down Main Street, posing this question in my spirit to my Father. Like a huge morning sky, my heart filled with such deep love. I no longer feared delivery, motive and failure.

In fact, I didn't see myself at all. I saw how more freedom and power could be opened up to someone I love so much.

But speaking the truth in love, we are to grow up in all aspects into Him who is the head, even Christ, from whom the whole body, being fitted and held together by what every joint supplies, according to the proper working of each individual part, causes the growth of the body for the building up of itself in love. (Eph 4:15-16)

I now ached to go to her, to share what I was seeing, gently and openly, without concrete declarations that left her out of her own story. I wanted to offer my identity to another, to show up for His body, to be the piece I am—not for me, but for my whole Jesus family. I saw how my words could cause her to feel seen and deeply loved.

And she is.

LXXIV

If you are reluctant to acknowledge the beautiful qualities in the people around you, check your heart.

Withholding encouragement can be a passive-aggressive attempt to flex yourself against the shining revelation of Jesus in others,

simply because you dread feeling small in their shadow.

And yet, even as you flee insignificance, you have acknowledged that you are highly influential.

How else could you recognize that withholding your honor of someone else might have weight?

But in holding your tongue, you choose invisibility. Your silence makes insignificance your tragic reality. In silence, the great one makes himself small.

The truth is this: he who builds others is great.

LXXV

Our family talks a lot about being brave. Recently it has been a key topic for us, as both of our older kids have been overcoming specific fears.

In the car today, Dax was celebrating his victory, delighting in how brave he had been. For a minute I thought he might be mistakenly combining courage with sure success in his mind.

I wanted him to realize bravery can still result in failure, so that he would identify that courage is in trying again and again until victory comes. It's important for me and Nick that our kids don't fear failure.

So I asked him, "Dax, do you know what bravery really is? It's when you feel the fear..."

and he finished my sentence in his little boy voice: "...And you stand up to it! You run towards it!"

His purity and enthusiasm filled the space between us with light. I think he gets it—and honestly, I get it too.

LXXVI-C

LXXVI

As a child, I read *Farmer Boy* by Laura Ingalls Wilder. My dad had the book as a child, and when I found it, I must have read it several hundred times. The story took place in the 1860s in upstate New York. The author describes the sweet, golden butter that Mother would make. She would then store it in tubs in the cellar, under white cloths.

One day, as he did from time to time, the butter buyer came to the farm. He was a friendly man with a gold watch. He picked up his butter tester tube and went into the cellar with Mother. This tube was long and hollow with a slit on one side, designed to push through the visible surface of the butter and take a sample. The slit would expose the telltale streaks of lower-quality, paler-yellow butter deceptively hidden at the bottom of the tub.

He went tub by tub, shoving that long tester deep into each sample and examining them carefully. Each was full--top to bottom--of perfect, high-quality butter. No streaks.

The butter was worth fifty cents a pound—an unheard of price. Quality spoke for itself.

Every time I mull over the thought that our Father is good, I recall the good butter, examined all the way through and found to be without defect. This is His goodness to me—His superior quality. He is the definition of quality. He defines "good-ness." He *is* good, all the way through Himself. No streaks.

His goodness is not the same as His greatness. Greatness is a reflection of his breadth--how huge He is. Goodness to me

is a reflection of His depth; that every detail of Him is
without defect.

LXXVII

I was laying out the food for our picnic when my friend
came over. "Do you hear what the kids are saying?"

I turned and looked. Our children were playing in the
stream under the evening sun. It was a large stream, about 30
feet across, with a sloping entry on our side and a grassy
bank on the other. Our kids were wading and jumping and
exploring, but I couldn't hear them. "What are they
saying?," I asked.

She looked at me, her dark eyes twinkling: "Can you make it
to the other land?"

I looked again and saw that to our children, the laughing
stream was far wider than it was to us. The distant bank,
rising several feet from the water's edge, was "the other
land." As the night passed, we'd see a child or two reach that
side and stand triumphantly with broad smiles, clothes
dripping and face glowing.

I thought of how big my Father is. To Him, our oceans are
like simple streams and our lands much closer than we
perceive.

I have thought of that moment so many times since, when friends have shared their challenges and dreams. I think of it when I feel my own heart burn with hope. We tend to look ahead, to the unknown and its obstacles, through the scary crayfish and slippery rocks—but instead, I've begun to hear in my heart, "Can you make it to the other land?"

And now today's adventure seems like a friendly invitation instead of an intimidating risk. I'm seeing things according to how big He is.

To Him, oceans are pleasant streams and far-off lands much closer than they appear.

LXXVIII

Maturity is not what I know.
Maturity is how much I walk in what I know.

LXXIX
REJECTION

It hasn't happened yet.

I can smell him coming but it hasn't happened. Not yet.

But it will. I'm not prophesying, and this isn't hopeless self-pity. I'm just speaking from experience, and from that strong instinct women learn not to ignore. All the pieces are assuming the position.

I can smell him. You could even say I invited him, by taking a new risk.

It would be easier to bear if he would simply walk up to my front door and be honest about himself, but rejection has no integrity. No, he won't even be honest about himself. He will come to me with a cardboard face, pretending to be prettier than he is, formulating a story that leaks water like a broken bucket.

Rejection hates me because I know the name of resurrection. How many times has he plowed me over and enjoyed my tears, only to watch in horror as Love raises me again?

There is a silver lining in watching rejection saunter up to me with his jeering smile—the moment when he realizes I no longer care what he thinks.

LXXX
BROKEN BONES

Let the bones which You have broken rejoice. (Ps 51:8)

Last summer, my Father broke me. On purpose. I didn't see it coming. I didn't think I deserved it, didn't understand it and definitely didn't handle it well. For a while I considered it the cruelest thing I had ever endured, as the wound was delivered to a place in which I was already terribly vulnerable.

Often when Nick gets home from work, we'll connect in the kitchen while I pull together some form of dinner. The kids clamor to tell their stories but we are pretty firm that they wait until he and I have had a chance to download whatever is stirring inside of us.

In the months following last summer, many many of those times, he would hold me together as I worked through all the emotions that were coursing through me. He has spent countless hours listening to me as I worked through anger, hurt, confusion, frustration and even when I considered walking away from it all. He is the reason I did not quit. He simply wouldn't let me.

It's not that I'm a quitter. I was just hurting inside. More than I ever had. I didn't know if I was strong enough to hold up under it. But I knew that this was of the Father.

I knew it was Him.

I knew I was learning more about
who He really is

how He really loves
who I really am
what that really looks like.

And my hope that He could bring it full circle was the only thing I had to hold on to. I didn't see how it could ever be anything but painful. But as the days wore on, His was the only outcome I could wait for, the only finish line I had enough faith for.

Oh, I begged for it to end. To be shorter. To make sense.

But at some point I stopped wishing for it all to be over, and surrendered to the belief that Love would be faithful to me. I leaned into His covenant with me. I learned to live with the gaping black hole in my heart–knowing that the Father knew it was there, and would be faithful to heal it when it was time.

I kind of learned to live around it.

Today, midafternoon, I felt it heal.

I felt it. In the place where there was a black hole, a total void of love, an absolute emptiness… suddenly I felt it flood full. I stopped what I was doing and froze, startled and at full attention for several minutes as it tangibly, physically resurrected inside of me.

When Nick got home, it was the first thing that poured out of my mouth. I had felt my heart heal. I had felt it! As I shared the details, he celebrated, pouring me a glass of water. When he looked up, I told him what I had said to the Father, the moment I felt it. I told him what I whispered: "Oh, NO."

I was afraid. I had learned how to live around the void, that ugly hole. I had learned how to speak around the lump in my throat, the twinge that was constantly with me. I had developed accommodations that allowed me to be in relationship without feeling it inside. I had embraced constant sadness. It's not that I developed walls; it's that the hole made me numb, and with numbness came insulation.

But now, I am feeling again.

The house has grown quiet and I'm sitting here asking my Father questions, the "how" questions, the "give-me-the-rules-and-specifics" questions, the safety zones to arm me, to maneuver through love without risking another Last Summer.

He's not interested in seeing me retreat into immaturity. Hows and rules are so Last Summer.

In His genius, I've be reborn in the days, weeks and months since Last Summer. I barely endured it, not realizing that He wasn't destroying. He was remodeling. Tenderly selecting, polishing, rubbing and caressing me in His unbroken faithfulness. *May the bones which you have broken rejoice!* When he put me back together, He assembled me among the very fibers of Himself.

I no longer need hows and rules. All that I need, He already gave. The confidence, faith and joy that are rising from the ashes are the beautiful features in my upgrade.

And the vulnerable spot that He broke? It is immeasurably stronger.

There's still a lump in my throat. It's still unnatural to feel this much and to choose not to hide it.

I could still really royally screw this up all over again.

But I feel His breeze on my face...

LXXXI

A friend recently asked me a good question in a tone of sad frustration: "Why don't people tell their stories more?"

After years of feeling alone, she had recently heard stories that helped her own shame and struggles feel less punishing.

I offered her a good answer, but truthfully, I woke up this morning unrested about it; instead I saw how my Father thinks about our testimonies.

A testimony is, by definition, a story of how the love of Jesus overcame within us. It is evidence of Him, proof of His love, current, potent and alive.

Telling our story is never just telling *our* story. Our story is *His*, and it belongs to all.

This week I overheard: If one breaks through, we all break through.

We overcome by the Blood of Jesus and the Word of our Testimony.

To suffer in silence and overcome in silence does not seem in Kingdom order. To closely guard our personal Jesus victories is to lay down one of the primary weapons in our arsenal.

Father is our wisdom, teaching us what and how to share.
Holy Spirit is our prompter, offering opportunity.
Jesus is our example, modeling what it is to lay ourselves down.
Family is our platform: they need us to walk openly with them.
Grace is abundant, empowering us to rise to His way, and
Love is our reason. We partner with Jesus that all may overcome.

If we understood the kindling fire of hope that our chests contain, we would open it for access at every good opportunity.

LXXXII

Honesty is not always an accurate representation of reality, as much as it's an open presentation of perception.

Honesty is good. But if we demand respect for honesty that bears false witness and reinforces strongholds, we miss out on the opportunity to heal and grow.

So yes, sure, let's be honest. It's important. But don't stop there. Let's submit our honesty to the Father's reality so it can become something true and real and strong.

When we humbly allow Father to challenge our perceptions, we open ourselves to panoramic viewpoints unhindered by our past.

Our allegiance is not to honesty for the sake of rawness---but to truth, for the sake of identity.

LXXXIII
ASK THE QUESTION

I believe I ensure wisdom's constant flow into my life when I receive her well. Wisdom knows her worth and loves to know she is valued. What is the best way to receive wisdom when she speaks, so that she knows I value her?

I think I have tried every possible approach.

When wisdom has spoken to me, I have:

- hurried to explain that I already knew of this wisdom––totally blind that I did not.

- discarded it entirely. Because I distrusted or dishonored the person who gave it, I did not consider their voice to be wise.

- absorbed it without discernment, anxious to win the approval of the person who gave it.

- nodded as though I grasped the words, and ignored the questions in my heart that signaled that I did not understand.

- been fretful that my counselor would see me with shortcomings, more preoccupied with my reputation than my becoming.

- turned an deaf ear, more focused on being able to tell my story than to actually glean the wealth of another.

- postured myself to immediately respond, cutting its voice short in my reluctance to submit or be vulnerable.

- considered myself unworthy or not qualified of the answer, so I did not ask the real question. I've also avoided the question in the fear of embarrassment, stubbornness that I was right or could figure it out on my own.

- fought back, because the counsel was hitting hot buttons that I resented, or because I wanted to demonstrate having a mind of my own. It seemed that a good push back would show I was thinking for myself, even if I knew eventually I would let them see I knew they were right.

- piously disdained the counsel, walking as a nomad from the family that polishes us to perfection.

I have also permitted something I considered prophetic to be exempt from wisdom, but of course it never is. *The fear of the Lord is the beginning of wisdom…*

All of these, and probably more, have surfaced as those who love me counsel me.

It seems that wisdom will always encounter my flesh when she speaks to me, as she carries the very equipment to strengthen my spirit, my identity, and my life. My flesh is the defeating force that will always attempt to neutralize her power when she speaks. And if you look closely above, you will see flesh attempting to inject her poison in every instance.

Does not wisdom call,
And understanding lift up her voice?
On top of the heights beside the way,
Where the paths meet, she takes her stand;
Beside the gates, at the opening to the city,
At the entrance of the doors, she cries out!... (Proverbs 8)

I have much to learn, but what I have learned is this: it matters little that wisdom is crying in the streets if my heart is not open to hear her.

Haven't we all had the counselor, the well-meaning one, come to us––and we hardened? Haven't we all encountered the wise voice that we did not welcome? We have resented them, filtered them, silenced them, ignored them, disqualified them, belittled them––and in every case, we revealed our own heart.

Imagine the inner turmoil this causes for those among us with great insight and few who will really listen. Do you think they can't sense the rejection, the subtle glaze that casts across our eyes as we tune out? To know the pent-up burst of gold that would release if we would only pause long enough to call upon it? There are many among us with great Wisdom alive within them. To treat this wealth with contempt is heartbreaking.

Imagine the agony of knowing you could bring clarity, vision, healing and wholeness in broad strokes, if only someone would listen? Imagine how you might, over time, learn to hold your tongue, waiting with baited breath for a searching one to come and sit with you. Imagine the appetite you would have for the one who comes, and instead of voicing their complaint, and lamenting their malady... instead of consuming the air of the room with confusing gloom, they open a silent moment to your voice.

And open their hearts to living Light.

Want to signal your thirst for wisdom? Ask a question.

Really, honest-to-goodness, on purpose--turn your heart to Wisdom. Open your heart and seek out someone who is harvesting the fruit you long for. Set aside your pride; arrogance and wisdom are mortal enemies. Lay aside your fear, that imagined foe. Dismiss all allegiance to hopelessness and inevitable defeat. Give up all white-knuckled claim to what you already know and allow wisdom to shape it anew. Allow understanding to make new connections; her simplicity is a sharp spade that will allow your roots to go deeper.

Seriously, half of the battle is asking the question. It accomplishes the internal work—the respect and honor you pay in ensuring your soil is ready for new seed.

Asking the question is not required for wisdom to speak, but it signals that my heart is uniquely open and vulnerable to the answer. It demonstrates humility has silenced ego and rebellion. And best of all, it reveals that the heart is soft and fertile.

So ask the question. And then listen to the answer.

Really listen. To the full answer. Go and put in motion her simple counsel. You will invite the storehouses of Abundant Life Himself into your reality.

LXXXIV

Ok, so part of learning to be one with my husband is deciding to come into agreement with him when I DO NOT AGREE.

He does this for me, too.

And it has taken WORK and SUBMISSION and BITING MY TONGUE...

...and TRUSTING and TRYING AGAIN and SHARING BLAME.

Turns out, it's rarely really about the issue.

I've been surprised so many times. It will produce the fruit we hope for, if the seed we've sown is unity.

LXXXV

At some point, sons have to take what they've experienced and allow love to etch it on their hearts. It has to become real. It has to breathe in your chest.

What you've experienced of others, what you've seen in yourself—at what point will you contend for your Father's ideas to become your unshakeable perspective?

Conflict is the gift that transfers our emotional encounters into faith-driven identity. Conflict sets fire to anything not rooted in the Vine.

This is a good thing. This is love manifested. This is life contending for victory within you.

Don't run from conflict, but know where the real battle is waged. Don't fear emotions; challenge them to come into the light. Just stand, rejecting any instinct for retreat.

Stand on quivering knees if you must.

Let Love prove Himself right there in the middle of the maelstrom.

When Love proves Himself, He confirms you within yourself, the last doubter.

...And let endurance have its perfect result, so that you may be perfect and complete, lacking in nothing. (James 1:4)

...After you have suffered for a little while, the God of all grace, who called you to His eternal glory in Christ, will Himself perfect, confirm, strengthen and establish you. (I Peter 5:10)

LXXXVI

That moment you shamefully hang your head before the throne of your Father because you know He knows how nasty that fridge was. He knew about the goo that was hiding behind the coconut flour and how old those limes were.

You thank Jesus for the cross and promise forevermore that living in His name will include the crisper drawers. You resolutely lay your hand on your cookbooks and swear to uphold the integrity of cheese.

He doesn't mention including the State of Oven in the deal, so you gratefully don't mention it either.

Because that's a whole 'nother stone to roll away.

LXXXVII

After a recent trek of errands, we were carrying a bunch of bulky things into the house from the van. Dax wanted something heavy, so I found a suitable box and settled it into his arms.

I watched him stagger under the weight for a moment then quietly asked, "Is it too much?"

His body language rejected my question. "I am strong!" he declared between breaths. "Nothing can beat me!"

With that, he muscled the box up the front steps, let it thud on the living room floor, and bounded outside for another load. The job was soon done and Dax's shoulders were bright with confidence.

Earn your own respect. Carry more than you think you can.

LXXXVIII
THE REAL REVOLUTIONARIES

If a director were to cast the role of a revolutionary,
they would begin with characteristics that the camera
understands.

Perhaps a broad-shouldered reluctant with a muscular
posture and a kind but graveled voice.

He mustn't be chubby, lest he be comical (or worse:
pathetic).
He mustn't be scrawny, lest he lack command.
He mustn't be old, lest he appear impotent.
He mustn't be young, lest his naiveté call up our contempt.
Above all, he mustn't be ugly, lest women reject him.

Perhaps the typecast is even more damning if a woman is
called.

Unless she be trim and witty, with straight teeth and perfect
breasts (which, incidentally, we see just enough of), all
wrapped in a hypnotic disdain for authority, our vision is
sunk before it is even launched.

When it comes to powerful women, we know what we
want to see.

We know that revolutionaries are nothing if not believable.
So first the hero is cast, so that the eye will buy.

It is easily formulaic, and we buy. Over and over, until we
no longer recognize the true revolutionaries when we meet
them.

But the persistent market for the tale shows us with perfect evidence: we ache to truly join the revolutionary. Given the right cause, we would commit to the death.

And we have met them. And they far exceed the script we have been sold. I was convinced of this again today, as I spoke with them on the phone or stood in their presence.

Lest you mistrust me, I am not assigning the title of Revolutionary lightly, and these ones I write of would prefer I not assign it at all. They have submitted themselves to the place of the lowest servant, quite simply spending their entire energies on loving—without regard to sin, wealth, religion or position. This lifestyle is constantly challenged, even outright criticized, for there is not a world structure in existence that will survive it. Without rank and title, how we will know who is unimportant? The opposition to them would seem insurmountable—were it not for the gleeful awareness that it has already been defeated.

But who would dare elevate the least? Who would willingly spend themselves entirely upon people who are without power, without consequence, without influence, without importance? Who are they who actually see the marginalized, much less value and honor them? Who would repeatedly sow where fruit continues to resist? This seems not the work of revolution, but of insanity.

Surely there exists some sort of end, in which this foolish demonstration culminates in common sense that knows office hours?

No. Among these revolutionaries, love never fails.

And so every single day, wherever the feet of these fathers and mothers fall (for indeed, there is not one they fail to adopt), the boundaries of fear that would try to control or measure love are relentlessly conquered.

Among these ones, one standard exists: Jesus.

Perfect love is truly casting out fear–first from within the very hearts of these revolutionary lovers, and then in the tremor of their steps among us. First from hearts, and then from the very earth itself. Everywhere they go, orphans are dug from the wreckage.

These are the real revolutionaries. Every word they speak is Spirit and life. They defy damage and scars of their pasts by walking in Living Health Himself. They forsake their boundaries with loving, guarded hearts. They resent any idea that mystery persists, knowing their Father happily reveals every secret. They are so accessible that no one seems to notice when they have gone days and weeks without sleep. From their core, despite every expense, it emanates: let them come to Him in me!

And the world, true to the echo and shadow of Jesus in these places, is changing. Just as Jesus always said that it would. With love like this on the move, how could it not?

LXXXIX

There are many trains of thought that can trick us into allowing distance, disconnect and even dissolution into our relationships.

But the cure for all lies is consistent: just stay. Love them like you made a covenant to.

Stay when you don't feel like it, don't want to, or don't understand.
Stay when you're angry.
Stay when they screw up or when you screw up.
Stay in their lives and hold fast the ties.
Stay when the inspiration to stay has faded.

Love that purposefully stays has powerful properties. It eventually and completely ejects bitterness, envy, control, anger and insecurity from our insides. Love that stays is not just for them. It's for us, too.

Love that stays heals us all.

XC

Walking by the Father's Spirit demands that we trust our heart. The things of the Spirit require faith and courage, and only a trusted heart can nourish them.

If we mistrust ourselves, our perceptions of the Father will be warped, clouded and incomplete. If we trust ourselves, even our mistakes lead us deeper into knowing Him.

XCI

The innermost desires of our heart are never served by bitterness and self-pity. If they knock, do not let them into you.

XCII

It can seem we spend a long time healing.
It can seem we endure a long time remembering.
It can feel like a skin
long too hidden
long too afraid
now conspicuous and unnatural in the light.

It can seem we wake up
and lay down again
in the same state of middle
for far too many days.

But there are moments along the way
brilliant clicks of yes

where we become alerted
that something within
a thing persistently troublesome to death
has remembered to breathe and feels
right.
fitted, like the skin we were knitted in.

And worship aches from our innermost,
to see Him
to know Him as Completer
in faithfulness for that which has seemed to take too long.

These moments are holy communion.
There is sacred silence,
relief
and eye contact with eternity.

It can seem we spend a long time remembering our skin until the moment of suddenly.

The suddenlies are worth our patience.
The suddenlies are worth the price.

XCIII
THIS ONE'S FOR MY BROTHERS

I grew up with sisters. I didn't even have many male friends in my childhood. But in the last five years or so, I have somehow collected a huge assortment of brothers.

I have smart brothers and goofy brothers. I have philosophers, teddy bears and gladiators. I have visionaries, rock stars, fathers, geeks and globetrotters. Some of them make me laugh so hard that life has become much less serious. I have one brother so tall that when he hugs me, my arms go around his waist like a kid sister. Another always seems to show up at my shoulder when I need him. Each time, no fail, there he is.

Like a kid sister, time in a circle of my brothers changes me. Some of them push me past my comfort zone or mock when my girlishness is obviously hypocritical. Some carry me as part of their heart. Some laugh at my emotional processing, roll their eyes at my long writings, are deliberately gross and push my buttons just because they can.

But I'm often overwhelmed when I think about them. *Jesus, thank you for all my brothers.*

My brothers, in all their variety and style, brought a lot of fullness and dimension to my life. For all their torment, they also love me. They listen to me, value me, and fiercely protect me. They are bad-ass and they're puddles. They lower their shields and let me see, really see, their soft gooey centers. They sharpen their swords at my side, never viewing me with condescension.

My brothers have been instrumental in discovering my place as my Father's daughter. My brothers are the steel His love is built of. They lay a foundation of authority and strength to everything I do.

Sometimes I see how hard it is for them to be strong in a world that wants them to be feminine. All too often, I see their power rejected and their authority shamed. They are constantly doing battle with judgments that they're despots, misogynists or dispassionate. Any time they want to rein in drama, mete out justice or reset cultures, they are charged. When they want to do war, they are criticized that their swords are too sharp. I've seen their command resented and their discipline ignored, hamstrung at every turn by society's broken understanding of masculinity.

That's hard for them, when they really just need someone to believe in them and tell them to get in the ring and land some punches.

I'm ready to see more of my brothers bloodied from war without the steady whine that they be diplomats. I'm ready for us to give them some room to rise up well, without cutting them down every time they fail. I'm ready for them to fight, to roar from their chests. I want to see Jesus enter the room on their strong shoulders and righteous hearts. I'm ready to see the shadow of evil fade in their light. I'm ready to see them walking home from the field with their spirits fully alive and flying.

I'm ready to see what comes out of them when we actually trust them, fighting with them instead of against them.

This weekend, a friend of mine prophesied over the men among us and I felt these words: prime the pump.

I close with this, for my brothers, and I'm almost begging: Prime the pump. I really need to hear more of you. When you speak, when you take your place, when you fearlessly stand, when you hold your throne, it empowers me. It gives me open opportunity for my femininity.

I realize you might be out of practice, unsure what that looks like, or afraid of the cost, but let me be frank: too bad. We need kings. The queens need you. I need you (and sisters get to be bossy). What first comes out of you might be rough or ugly, but what will come afterward is worth that practice. Prime the pump. Open up and let your power flow out. Take your places.

Don't wait for permission. Don't wait to be nominated. I really can't wait to see what it looks like. I really can't wait for you to see how important you are, to understand how strong you make us, how much security and power you give us.

My brothers are mighty kings in the light of the King.

Thank you for being my brothers.

XCIV

Hunger for the Father will take us through places that
dissolve our strength. Hunger is strength for the wilderness.

He is kind to lead us into wildernesses.
He is kind to teach us the strength of weakness.
He is kind to allow our hearts to be galvanized in testing.
He is kind to activate our unfiltered sonship in the choking
vacuum of hunger.

When we look around in our spirit,
and all we see is barren landscape,
we remember that Jesus passed this way too.

We are walking in His footprints.

How deeply we must be loved,
How important we must be,

to be invited to walk the wilderness.

Wisdom teaches us to pray well during these times.

Pray for His kingdom.
Pray in who you know He is (regardless of how that is being
tested.)
Pray for His body.

Detach yourself from old ways and let your heart relearn its
roots. Guard your lips from complaint and keep your heart
from doubt. Be faithful and call up your faith.

Hold. Pass the test.

Trust Him. He is a genius Father. He is perfect faithfulness.
He who leads us into the wilderness is faithful to lead us out.

XCV

I wanted to say it
but thought
"They're too busy
for this small thing.

"I will hold my tongue and
treat them with great reverence
and save them from my small thing
that will most assuredly be
a silly distraction
from their great, important work."

Little did I realize
it's wasn't the thing I judged as small,

but me I bullied as small,

stuffing my generous heart into
a convenient, silent box
of inferiority
masked as restraint.

Disconnected
and forced apart
because I considered my silence more valuable
than my presence.

XCVI
VICTORY LAP

Last night, I was awake too long.

I had momentarily considered staying up all night, wrestling like Jacob, praying through my pain, but I remembered my morning-glory children, so I stubbornly drew a boundary on my fretting.

I saw midnight....1am...2am... until I finally could shut down my mind long enough to roll over and fall asleep.

I could probably employ some great wordsmithing here to paint a dramatic picture of the emotional vortex I was working through, but honestly, there's just no value in it. Maturity has taught me to put all the frayed pieces of "miscellaneous angst" in the Jesus fridge until He pulls them out and shows me their origin, flavor and purpose.

Women like to dive into the details of the feelings, but let's avoid that particular ditch, shall we? There is a higher thing to see here.

I laid there, stranded between too much caffeine, too many unchallenged vain imaginations, too much winter and a little too much loneliness. I knew I could awaken Nick and he would listen, but I just couldn't make myself nudge him. He's always available, but if he woke me from a dead sleep to talk about his feelings, I would ~~probably~~ definitely slug him. It only feels right to respect his sleep accordingly.

So I laid there, swirling.

I prayed and I slowed my mind down as much as I could manage. I took inventory and sorted, piece by piece, all the different fragments inside, knowing the truth of Jesus in each place would establish peace. I turned my heart toward difficult relationships and opened myself to thinking past what was obvious or convenient. I shut down every lie I found. I got a midnight text from a night-owl friend and opened my heart just enough so she could see a glimpse and be in prayer with me.

But I was tired, and the climb was steep. I ended the spin with an iron-fisted distraction, and fell asleep.

When I awoke, I felt clear for the first thirty seconds. My rested morning mind felt foolish to have spiraled in the dark. I chuckled, bemused and relieved to leave the fuss as memory. But within moments, the storm came spinning back and I felt my heart sink.

I fought tears for the next two hours, in pain and exhausted from the battle within.

But then, as though the sun had pierced black clouds, authority dawned in my heart. The pain had tapped a vein that bled gold. I stood up on shaky feet and told the storm to be still.

There was pensive stillness for several hours. The Spirit was brooding over me, teaching me.

Eventually a memory from last weekend crept forward. Our family was in the van together and Nick was talking with the children about life skills that take a lot of focus and failure to develop, but eventually we can do them without really even thinking about it.

Example: walking. He told them how they had been as toddlers, with their pudgy, faltering steps and frequent bottom-down thuds. *But do you think about walking now, or do you just do it?* he asked them. *We just do it,* they replied.

I thought of the storm I had so recently walked through, and I marveled.

I don't have nearly as many of these emotional storms as I used to. I was once easily tossed around by my emotions. But I had been planted in a place designed to challenge and call up my identity, forging my sonship from theory to reality. That process triggered what was easily thousands of blinding blizzards of emotions and confusion.

I had countless nights in front of this computer screen, weeping and writing and feeling, without any sense of what was real or imagined. Truthfully, I didn't know up from down for years. Had I not been well-loved, I never would have persevered.

Disciplining our emotions is difficult skill to learn. Especially for a woman. I needed to harness the emotions that would sabotage my identity without deadening the instincts that empowered my femininity.

I needed a real knowledge of my Father that superseded anything I felt, so that He could instruct my heart clearly and powerfully in the middle of opposing evidence.

I needed to be able to feel pain yet unwaveringly trust Him, so that my faithfulness and unity would never be vulnerable to my pain.

I needed to be my Father's daughter when I didn't feel like it.

It took experiencing, and then rightly leading, my every emotion. There was a lot of silence, submitting to the fire of letting all of it be challenged and rearranged. It took wanting to be free more than I wanted to be validated.

It was brutal and exhilarating.

I looked at last night anew, seeing that I didn't plunk down on my toddler backside this time.

But shouldn't I have been able to shut down the storm and walk on top of it? Should I have been able to tell my heart to be still? Should I have been able to do that faster?

Yep. Sure. That would have been good.

But I couldn't, at least not right away. It was a big twisted mess, and I'm still growing. And that's OK. I'll get more chances to get stronger, to grow in the elegant grace of a unfretful daughter.

But I'm choosing to celebrate the areas of victory, because there were some:

- I did not send fretful texts that inflated my emotions, nor did I try to rationalize my emotions into something holy or intercessory, when they were not.

- I did not let my emotions keep me awake all night, draining energy from the next day.

- I did not have any self-righteous conversations with people who were not in the room, projecting them as villains and myself as a victim.

- I did not fight by flesh, neither with control mechanisms nor by temper tantrum.

These are all things I have done so often in the past, the panicked survival strategies of a heart afraid to break. Habits that broke when Love healed my fear.

I realize this is a weird victory lap.

But I think it's important to see these times well: to celebrate the wins, to embrace the pain, and to humble ourselves to where we have room to grow. If I don't look well at the things He walks with me through, I'll miss realizing how big His grace was. I'll overlook the marvel of Him, and the personal way He walks with me.

This isn't about knowing the Father in theory. It's about building something real with Him that capitalizes on every imagination He has of us together. It's about becoming a powerful and personal manifestation of who I have experienced Him to be.

When we see well, we become convinced of His goodness. We heal deeply. Our hearts marvel and grow. Our faith increases and we become bold.

We stand higher, we see further, and we do not fall down as quickly.

We have wins to celebrate. We have a testimony to reveal. We write a victory story that can be offered as hope for those still learning to overcome.

I don't care if it takes me five minutes or five days or five weeks or five years to finally find my feet on top of the waves. Every inch of that climb taught me about His heart and showed me the progress we're making together.

Progress is victory.

XCVII

If, in my heart, I hear the cry,
"But that's not fair!"
I can be certain I am operating in unbelief,
living as a mortal.

And if, in my heart, I carry that cry to Jesus,
trusting Him to be my reward,
He perfectly renews my mind and secures my identity.

When He is my source, I am able to contend for what is just.

XCVIII

Tonight, our family was in the backyard. We had decided to transform an old flowerbed into an herb garden, so a gnarled collection of creeping shrubs had to be pulled out. They were deeper than we imagined and the job was harder than we'd gauged.

Once the larger pieces were removed, we worked together to comb through the soil for any remaining roots. We started talking to the kids about roots, and how our hearts are like soil. Jesus digs up ugly roots in our hearts and makes room for good things to grow.

With their fingers soiled and chests heaving, they easily followed our words. We asked them what they thought bad roots might be, and they said things like fear, lying and disobedience.

Then we looked for good roots—good things that grow big in our hearts—and they said beautiful things like love, honesty and strength.

Nearly finished, we discovered a stubborn root. I said, "Aly, give that a hard tug. You can do it. It's a bad root. Let's pretend it's a lie. Pull that bad thing up!"

She bent down to try and suddenly, light dawned on her face. "Strength!" she exclaimed. And giving it a double-portion of determination, she ripped the root from the soil.

My heart was bursting as we finished planting herbs in the ready soil. Far more valuable than these plants was the beautiful soil working next to me, her hands and knees caked with mud, her eyes bright with understanding about her good heart and how Jesus strongly tends her.

XCIX

I have spent enough of my life being suspicious and skeptical and judgmental of my leaders. I see the memes, I read the comments, and I ache over the partisanship. I have resisted and moaned and despaired.

But since I started praying for them,
my heart changed.

I see possibility and opportunity. I respect how smart they are and I see what isn't reported. I can discern the merit of their ideas and appreciate their work.

I trust my leaders. My Father established them, and I trust Him.

Therefore, in my allegiance to Jesus, my heart can operate in pure, powerful trust and prayer alongside those who carry the weight of leadership.

C

I heard the words and they were accurate. But something came with the words that unsettled my heart.

The spirit of the thing is more important than the thing.

We went to see the movie and it was good. But as we left the theater, heaviness and emptiness lingered in the air like a dissatisfying aftertaste.

The spirit of the thing is more important than the thing.

I donated money to the cause that was important to me. A week later, I read a recent interview with the head of that foundation. His words carried a murky, unworkable arrogance. Mysteriously, I regretted giving my support.

The spirit of the thing is more important than the thing.

She seemed gentle, but I sensed anger...
His words were right, but there was no love in them...
I said it, wishing I meant it...
They all seemed fine with it, but I just couldn't shake an uneasiness...

The spirit of the thing is more important than the thing.

Things that are of the Father carry both the words and the Spirit of Truth. If the spirit is off, pause. Pray. Seek out His reality—in spirit and truth. No one who waits on the Lord is put to shame.

The spirit of the thing is more important than the thing.
– Mark Durniak

CI – CXIX

CI

The world teaches us to expect unfaithfulness... to brace ourselves for disappointment and broken relationship.

After a while, unfaithfulness becomes the foggy lens by which we view all relationships.

This means that during inevitable times of weird distance or lack of communication, we think that relationships have dissolved, that affection has faded, or that commitments have eroded because our emotions are full of insecurity and confusion.

Someone doesn't respond to our messages, relate with us the way we wish they would, or affirm us like we feel they should, and we begin to draw conclusions.

We build sandcastles of our disappointments, founded in the inaccurate discernment of a worldly mindset.

And because of how we see, because of how we allowed the world to program our thinking, we actually become the thing we thought we saw. In our hearts, we become unfaithful...because we thought they were.

We react to the thing we think we see, instead being the Father's son in faithfulness and truth to what is.

But Jesus is the perfect source to sustain our faithfulness when the ones we love aren't fueling our staying power.

Lies will erode the foundations of our relationships. We should be suspicious of any thought that creates distance in our heart toward others.

Division is a two-way agreement, a partnership of fear.

So it is up to our response. We check our hearts and ask: Who are they? What do I know about them? What is the truth? Am I holding them accountable as food for something hungry in me?

In forcing truth to arise in our heart, we cling fast to our brother, and remain faithful to them at all costs.

Faithfulness looks at the opportunity for division

and chooses truth instead.

CII

Home is our Father.
Family, in its purest form, is wholly contingent on Him as our foundation.

We can try to pursue our idea of family
apart from abiding in Him as our home,

Trying to be for one another what He must be.

But at best it will be dissatisfying
And at worst, toxic.

Home is Dad.
Family is the pure expression of His love.

CIII

Love clearly counsels us in wise flexibility---advising us on the sacrificial Yes and the righteous, guilt-free No.

CIV

What we believe about God determines how we live.
So how does God think about time?

Is He able to redeem years that were lost or wasted?

Is He the same God who stopped the sun at Joshua's word?

As His sons, do we misuse the phrase "I didn't have time?"

When we feel rushed or forced against our spirits, have we stepped out of His rest and authority?

When time does not work in our favor, do we seek His fingerprints in the disruption? Do we stand before His face and seek His wisdom?

Is it a lie that time is beyond our authority?
Can sons learn to flex the constraints of time?

CV

If the prodigal came home to his father on a Sunday, I wonder what Monday was like.

During the night, the servants burned his disgusting, tattered clothes, carrying them from the house at arm's length, faces distorted from the smell.

His big brother was up with the dawn, freshly appreciative of his father's estate and his place in it.

His father, who had tossed sleeplessly for months and had worn a face of lined pain, woke with new ideas. He was the first one to the breakfast table. The table was quickly strewn with his plate on his left and plans on his right, eyes still on the horizon but now with vision.

The whole household hummed in the early morning twilight, each with a curious eye on that bedroom door. Everyone heard the bed creak as the wanderer awoke.

On Sunday a prodigal. Last night a party and a homecoming. On Monday...what? What would he be?

Only the prodigal could answer that question.

Would he choose to rise early like the heir would, to pick up his identity and his weight?

Would he open himself to learn the ways of his father?

Was home his last resort or his restoration?

Would he make the jump from prodigal to prince?

Every prodigal has a Monday morning.

CVI

Above all, keep fervent in your love for one another, because love *covers a multitude of sins.* - I Peter 4:8

My brothers, if any among you strays from the truth and one turns him back, know that he who turns a sinner from his wandering will save his soul from death and will *cover a multitude of sins.* - James 5:19-20

Two of Jesus' friends, Peter and James.
Both with authentic knowledge of Jesus use the exact same Greek phrase.

But Peter says that love covers sin.
James says that contending for one another is key.

Two brothers eminently qualified
Two sons entirely trusted
to describe how sin gets covered.

So what covers a multitude of sins?

Love that turns one another toward the truth,
those who faithfully contend for one another,
family members who serve one another
laying aside anything less than the way of Jesus in all things.

Submitting to one another.
Laying down fear in favor of the higher thing:
the perfection of Jesus in every one of us.

Turns out that prolonged silence
or complacent indifference
toward one another's blind spots
are the opposite of love that covers.

Father, you are Love.
Just as you contend for us,
teach us to contend for each other.

CVII

Commitment built on emotion isn't commitment at all. It erodes when the storm inside us undermines our intentions.

"What's going on inside of me?" forces the storm to identify itself. It reveals insecurities, fears and weaknesses that require a new way of thinking.

The new way is rarely the change of someone else. It is often the change that is necessary within me.

Be born again in the spirit of your mind. Let love walk through the storm with you. Stand bravely, arms wide open to love, jaw set to the wind. Christ in you is the hope of glory!

When you learn to stand, you relearn what it is to commit.

Commitment rooted in love becomes stronger each time it weathers a storm. Storms galvanize identity and test commitment. It is there that unity can grow.

"What's going on inside of me?" – Mark Durniak

CVIII

A friend and I were discussing how creative we become when money gets low. And I began to wonder: Why is this? Why do I suddenly become motivated by lack when my identity is one of plenty? Why do I become creative only when my circumstances pressure me to?

I often I put my Father in an silly position: I say I want Him to bring me increase, but I really only supernaturally create it when I'm forced to.

Immaturity, I see you hiding in my shadows.

Setting aside my laziness and entitlement, I looked for open doors to create, instead of last-ditch outlets to survive.

The ability to make something out of nothing is in our DNA. Whether we flex these muscles is entirely up to us.

CIX

When I was teenager, I spent several months in perpetual tears. I would come home from school and Mom would pause her work to endure my dramatic (and I'm sure hormonal) weeping over my long list of grievances from the school day.

Eventually, she gave me some sober insight: "Dear, God put big things in your heart. If you want to walk in big things, you're going to have to endure big challenges."

I remember how those words landed inside me. I had barely begun to live, but I wanted to believe my life would matter. Her advice brought my tears to an end and infused my spine with steel. With her perspective came vision, and vision equipped my heart.

Mom knew I was strong, and knew how to communicate with me. She formed her words to offer the challenge I needed, as if to ask me: "How bad do you want it?"

Years later, after high school, I moved from my parents' home to Charlotte, North Carolina. There were new challenges to being on my own, and I heard those words from her again as we spoke on the phone one evening. Years after that, I heard them again when my marriage was troubled.

I've heard them only a handful of times: "If you want to walk in big things, you're going to have to endure big challenges." She saves them for the moments she knows I'm listening to hopelessness. My mom is tremendously wise.

It has come to be that now those words have grown into a fruitful tree in my heart. I don't always remember it is there, but today an apple from that tree rolled down the hill where I was huddled in a little ball.

I watched it roll up to my feet and come to a stop, its polished skin forming a mirror before me.

How bad did I want it? Would I stop here? Had I been conquered? Or would I again, in the model of Jesus, overcome? The big things in my heart--the brilliant ideas of Jesus...was I willing to let them die here, unsupported by the testimony of life in me?

It's funny how little a spark identity needs to remember its roar.

CX
RECOVERING FROM TRY

I am a recovering Try addict.

I don't know if I'm in recovery yet. Most days I still feel like my Try is still stuck in gear.

But the good news is that my Try is wearing out, like a tire nearly bald. So perhaps a crash is in my future. But I'm no longer afraid of it.

In fact, I would book a ticket for the nose dive if I could.

For a while, my response to the death of my Try was simply Try Harder. I haven't met many circumstances that couldn't be overcome by iron stubbornness. But please don't confuse stubbornness with faithfulness. Faithfulness is of the Father's Spirit sustained by trust. Stubbornness is what happens when the flesh kicks in to stay alive.

My stubbornness is fear.

Faithfulness is different. It is lion's blood in my veins. It is fiercely loyal to the manifested passions of Jesus in my heart.

The things I built with Try must be held together by Try Harder. They are crumbling.

Their end is in sight, and I must allow them to fall if I want to begin again.

I love my Father's Spirit.

Whose heart is open, let them listen carefully to what the Spirit says.

A surgery has begun and Jesus is cutting deep, to the seed of every branch within me. Many things are being severed, too weak to bear fruit or carry weight. They must be reborn.

Groan. *Again.*

These days, anything that requires Try depletes my tank immediately. So be it. My Father is teaching what I asked Him to show me. If not for the sinkhole within, I would never stop. I would Try until my knuckles bled and the bones showed through.

But Try is a lonely place. Try is how I muscle through alone, trying to prove what needs no proof.

The Holy One, the true one, who has David's key, who opens doors that none can shut and who closes doors that none can open.

If Jesus hasn't opened the door, it isn't open. No amount of pounding and pleading will melt the lock or change a mind. When Jesus opens a door, it is open. No power on earth can close it.

All I can do is open me. It goes against the Code of the Try'er. But it is the heart of the Lover.

I know all that you've done. Now I have set before you a wide-open door that none can shut.

Try is not the same as Work. Work is a valued tenant in my heart. I love work. I love to give my minutes to things that grow. I love to lay down spent on worthwhile pursuits.

Try is incompatible with self-love. It means I lay aside my core expressions out of a motivation to earn what can only be offered. Try attempts to sell me to buy you.

Try only lasts as long as human energy can sustain it. It results in loneliness because it reeks of insecurity.

How I am going to unlearn this? I have been Trying as long as I can remember.

Holy Spirit has placed at my heart a door, an opportunity, a call, a place that is truly mine. It exists for me. It wants me. It is why I am here. I don't have to contend for it. I only need to give myself to it. There are wide-open spaces to be explored. I can feel them.

Or at the very least, I'm hope I'm not crazy.

So cling tightly to what you have, so that no one may seize your crown of victory. For the one who is victorious, I will make you to be a pillar in the sanctuary of my God, permanently secure.

This is a "peace, be still" invitation of faith for my heart, for the recovering Tryer who is flat on her back, wiped out from years of pounding and whining at closed doors.

There is no more time to mourn the closed. There is only time to celebrate and pursue the wide open.

Starting with me.

References taken from Revelation 3 NASB

CXI

As long as I'm hell-bent on proving that my mistakes aren't my fault, I'm powerless to make effective changes.

CXII

True family can be a little disorienting for people who are used to having to pay their dues.

You can come to us for the first time and hang on the sidelines, thinking you need to feel us out, thinking you need to figure out how to ease into this big warm chaos...

not realizing you're already a part of us, already beloved by us, already wanted and needed. Tiptoe in if you need to, take your time if you must, but my goodness, please keep coming deeper.

We had no idea how much we missed you until we met you.

CXIII

Unrest
lack of peace
tells on itself.

Rest
Perfect Peace
reigns where He does.

There is no storm
the Prince and His truth
cannot calm.

If what I know of Him
if what I have always believed about Him
is not powerful enough
to overcome all without and within,

to proclaim "Peace Be Still!"
to heal, to restore, to supply,
to brilliantly declare His finished work,

if my thoughts are able to reason
against His goodness,

if reality seemingly rises to override Him,
to mock His weakness in my circumstances,

perhaps there is more of Him to know
than I have yet seen.

It is a verdict that
my understanding of Him
is incomplete.

If He is who He says He is,

all that we see and fear,
all that we mourn and criticize,
every barren, broken and poisoned thing within
must experience what He finished.

Instead of the arguments,
we must gently ask ourselves
(as one loved at the deepest part):
Is He King of this place?
Is He mine?

A thousand times yes,
and there fall the lines in pleasant places.

Perhaps anxiety
should be permitted
even commanded
to give an answer for its authority.

Perhaps instead of
wishing and pretending,
struggling in vain to bully a slave-driver,

we chase immunity by His Spirit.

We let His identity make us too slippery to hold.

We let the seeping clouds persuade us
to let go of the whip we have used
to beat ourselves
into a change than never comes

to lay ourselves into Love's hands

to ask for the revelation that convinces our hearts
that He is our good and kind King,
even here among the jagged rocks,

to trust Love to lead us
into an encounter of His Presence that builds our faith,
into an experience of His wild love,
into a confidence of His goodness

that forces worry and cruel imagination
to show the dull fangs of their foolishness.

Rest for the heart,
such that the winds cannot toss us,
is one of the great rewards of His heavens,
an outflow of being with Him.

Those who abide in the realms where Jesus lives
cannot be overcome.

He is Who He says He Is.
We are who He says we are.

CXIV

At one time in life, I was extremely opinionated and rarely hesitated to share what I thought.

But the spirit of my opinions was arrogant, absolute and shortsighted, publicly taking sides where I had no business declaring a position.

I had asked no questions.
I had nothing invested and nothing to lose.
I had no patience for the pain of others.
I was bold, cold and hard.
I was armed with empty principles, laws of sense and behavior that neither breathed or loved.

Noisy gong. Clanging symbol.

Wisdom isn't complicated. She isn't afraid to speak, and has a lot of things to teach us. She loves to weave His perspectives into our hearts and lives, and equip us to bring change.

But the Father's love first identifies where there are *people* stranded and tied within the cause, issue or conflict. His heart sees, heals and restores people.

Turns out that when people are genuinely, powerfully, individually loved, the issue tends to shift slowly into alignment with righteousness.

It's not that I don't have opinions. I do. But if I slaughter people or their reputations to communicate God's heart, I've missed it.

Here's His heart: People first. There's not a single one He's willing to throw away for the sake of a cause. Jesus already overcame. His sacrifice was enough.

May no more people die on our cross. May no more villains be named and maligned. It's just another lap around the blinded hearts who are crying out for us.

CXV

We messaged back and forth, carrying together a relationship my precious friend was aching over.

In a familiar flourish of tidiness (and with words I have echoed many times myself), she declared the date by which she hoped this person would overcome their challenges— neatly organizing a matter of the heart to a date on the calendar.

When I asked her to surrender her timeline, and instead, give this person God's full-on powerful, faithful love with patience and endurance—with no motivation to her own mental finish line—it was the most difficult thing I could have said to her. I cried with her; I have watched the ripped pages of my own plans flutter into the wind, my heart torn with them.

She came to me a few days later, still in the pain of laying down her deadline, in the heartache of denying her flesh the reasonable end she longed to force into reality. It was the plan that brought her strength; the dark tunnel for which she had drawn a door.

Erasing the door left only the tunnel, but the darkness was causing the Father's love in her to light up. She was so beautiful in that moment.

To love others in that way, without being subconsciously driven by what is sensible or fair, is fire in the veins. It demands the vital presence of Jesus. The flesh does not know how to love like that; only the Father can source such generosity.

But all victory, healing and change are found in the heart and Spirit. Only bold, true, long-suffering love takes us where we really want to go.

Mostly, our deadlines exist to indicate where we are pretty sure our grace on the subject is going to run out.

Love gets too expensive, it requires too much—and we get out our timeline.

By this day
By the end of the year
They're never going to get it
This again?
If this happens again…

Except Jesus has never loved us like that. While we were still entirely lost, He gave His entire self.

Living in the love that heals is the ridiculous business of superheroes.

Love puts light in the tunnel and helps those inside find their way out, holding our hand.

CXVI

So much of the pain of maturing is entirely avoidable.
He submits to my No.

He lets me opt out.

But for the joy set before me in Him,
for the hope of living wide open and entirely whole,
for the freedom and exhilaration of the horizons in His eyes

I choose Yes.

Even if that means I must go through pain sometimes.

I relax into His way of things.
I trust Him to measure the weight upon me.
I let Him take me through the eye of the needle,
the door through which only my original beauty will fit.

His entire heart for me is Life.
There is no death in His eyes concerning me.

Only that I would be fully alive.

Who can resist such single-minded attention and loyalty?
Why would I deny Him the rewards hidden in me?

Because His grace is in my shoulders,
the harder moments of growing up in Him
tend to remind me of how worthy He is of my all.

The struggle makes my love burn brighter.

I choose Him...in me...in Him.

The rest falls away, a shroud in which I no longer fit.

CXVII

"I know I should"
is often inwardly followed by
but I don't want to.

We do what we want to do.
We move the mountains we are motivated to move.

And "should" comes with a heavy yoke,
our soul feeling the trespassing coercion
of expectations we haven't met.

And there goes our creativity and our energy,
stoned to death by accusation.

Instead, may we offer our "shoulds"
before His eyes
for inspection.

If He says our name in His loving voice,
His wind bursting across our face,
does that "should" burn to ash?

Or does it spring to life
with brilliant leaves of soft green,

instantly transformed from "should"
to "want to."

Only Jesus knows which "shoulds" are real.
The rest are chains,
meant to slow us down.

Only Jesus knows which "shoulds"
mark the pathways of life
and which mark the gravestones of death.

CXVIII

Lies are never rooted in love.

Love has one definition: the Father.

His love is our one and only template.

His love is wise and able to discern the right time and place
for all knowledge. This discernment is the critical differential
between white lie and wise restraint.

His love is perfectly able to heal wounds and offense, and so
He is not afraid of them. But most of all, His love is unable
and unwilling to leave us incomplete.

I think sometimes we veil the truth because we are sourced
by an incomplete perspective of love. We fear the response,
doubt our own accuracy, commit to self-preservation, or
simply realize that we might do harm to those we have
affection for.

But we must be far wiser in how we carry the truth—the
truth we see in the Spirit, the truth of our own perspectives,
and the truth of how we really feel (right or wrong). I think
if we are not vigilant and discerning, we fall prey to a
powerless form of fake love that accepts silence over

transparency. In our desire to maintain peace, appear strong, or to protect others from pain, we foolishly allow distance—in the form of artificial unity—to keep us at arm's length from one another.

This sows mistrust, immaturity and contempt into relationships that the Father deeply desires to see become intimate, challenging and life-giving.

Our relationships appear close but are not woven in truth and love to our hearts.

And we often know it, yet feel stuck in maintaining the sandcastle we've built because we know it's where our relationships are truly rooted. To allow the waves of the brave ocean to rinse away our friendly lies would be to risk homelessness.

So we live in sandcastles instead of real ones.

Speaking the truth in love stimulates growth. In us. In others. And in the bonds of brotherhood that unite us all together.

...But, speaking the truth in love, we are to grow up in all aspects into Him who is the head, even Christ... (Eph 4:15)

There is such need for us to be wise. To be truly discerning and unafraid, because of His grace. We need to be more loyal to intimacy than we are to fear.

Speaking the truth transplants our relationships from the sandcastle to the Throne Room.

CXIX
LIKE VAMPIRES IN THE SUN

I was littered.

Everywhere I looked,
mortar shells of suspicion had torn black holes in my
relationships.

Within me were toxic holes of offense toward many I said I
loved.

When Jesus saw this place
His eyes were kind but sad.

Here and there were the twisted walls I'd built,
a city of doom half constructed
and built on foundations of imaginary accusations,
hazards where Jesus stumbled when He came to find me.

When I saw his crucified feet patiently moving around
my many illusions and judgments
to carve a path to me,
my heart broke.

So I began excavating every cratered thing
over and over and over
opening my heart
quivering and shaking
standing and learning
failing and winning.

I'm making it sound like work

but truly,
Jesus did it.

My entire effort was to
stay open and not run.

When I caught myself arguing
with the imagined and invisible,
I repented immediately,
turned myself to Jesus and said,
Ok. This is You and me.

Let's tear this stronghold down.
Remind me about this precious person
and expand Your love in me for what is real.
Source this in me.
Show me where You are in this.
Discipline me. Search me.
Help me test my emotions and affix to You as truth.
I hide nothing. I fear no one.
I am beautiful and loved and highly valued.
This is You and me.
Let's talk.

I experienced extraordinary freedom,
and gentle clarity.

and yet, some places of me simply would not submit.

I laid them open to the light,
waiting for them to burn to ash like vampires in the sun.
Waiting to be loved, reproved, and rebuilt.
Waiting to be told where I was wrong,
where I had faltered,
what needed fixing
so that I could heal
(so I could stop hurting).

I thought that if I could just get them to Jesus,
if I could just get these things to Him,
they'd come into context and lose their bite.

Surely they would burn to ash in His gaze and float away.

But there seemed to be pickaxe in my hands.

I seemed to be like a miner
slicing through black ore
and hitting solid rock.

The hammer clanged and recoiled.

And I could not figure out why these things
these firm unyielding tendons
these things embedded in me
would not yield to Jesus.

If anything, they became unspeakably pronounced,
immune to death.

I begged for their destruction.
I rejected them out of loyalty to Jesus.

But they refused to die.
They stood stubbornly within me,
as though constructed of immortal fibers
not consenting to dismissal.

And it dawned in me, *What if...*

... those things weren't meant to go?

After all this unreserved dismantling,
what if I finally hit the core?

What if these things would not die
because they were made of life?

Had I discovered the fortresses of Jesus?
Had I found my foundation?
Had I discovered something I could keep?

Covered in mud,
I leaned back and brushed my brow,
breathing hard,
streaks across my face.

I peered down,
testing and mistrusting
any idea that I would deliberately fail to
tear down my enemy.

But there it was,
peeking through the sediment.
A footer of solid gold,
grimed and gleaming.

I sat down,
sank back,
and wept.

ABOUT THE AUTHOR

Diane Helman is first, and most essentially, a daughter of the Lord: soft, strong and beautiful, in His image. From that place of simplicity and authority, she is wife to Nick Helman, her high school sweetheart and strong side. Along with three dynamic children (and all the dishes and laundry associated), they make their home in Chambersburg, Pennsylvania, United States, where they give themselves to the Father's kingdom, in relationships that extend throughout their community and the earth.

And while they have many ambitions and hopes for this life, their truest and deepest desire is that they would learn to love all well, in the way that Christ showed us.

LOVE. ALL. WELL.

Made in the USA
Middletown, DE
27 December 2018